ONE CHURCH, ONE LORD

John Whale

SCM PRESS LTD · LONDON

334 01184 1

First published 1979
by SCM Press Ltd
58 Bloomsbury Street, London WC1

Typeset by Gloucester Typesetting Co. Ltd
and printed in Great Britain by
Richard Clay Ltd
Bungay, Suffolk

ONE CHURCH, ONE LORD

TO THE COMPANY OF WORSHIPPERS
PAST, PRESENT AND FUTURE
AT THE PARISH CHURCH OF ST MARY
BARNES

Contents

List of illustrations

Preface

WHEN IN 1976 I BECAME RECTOR'S WARDEN OF THE
parish church at Barnes – a suburb of London some five miles
west of Hyde Park Corner, wrapped in a long bend of the Thames
– I was already an old journalist. As such, I found myself face
to face with a story. The rectors whom my predecessors had
served, I began to discover, were a very remarkable set of men.
They had taken a front-line part in home and foreign wars; they
had published voluminous calls to religious tolerance and intoler-
ance; they had been confidants and advisers to statesmen; they
had become bishops and scholars; they had known national
success in preaching sermons and writing hymns.

At first they seemed to me remarkable because their gifts
were out of scale with a perfectly ordinary parish church. But
then I saw that they might have a significance beyond that.
There is a well-understood journalistic device, much used both
in broadcasting and in newspapers, whereby the general is
represented not just by the particular but by a particular person.
Parliamentary overload is expounded through an account of
one backbencher's week; the Common Agricultural Policy is
made comprehensible in the life of a single farmer in Devon or
the Dordogne. I realized that – in the twenty-five rectors of a
single church between the Civil War and the Second World
War – I was fronted with a comparable opportunity raised to
the power of twenty-five. My rectors could tell the story of the
Church of England. They were all men of their time: their
eminence in their own day was enough to make sure that they
left vivid memorials behind them, yet not so towering as to stop
them being entirely typical. As a group, because they took

different sides in the same running arguments, they became hyper-typical. Laid end to end, their lives could constitute a serial biography of the English parson through three hundred years as he wrestled with all his most important concerns – doctrine, worship, church unity, church government, money.

The lives turned out to disclose a pattern. What they illuminated was the way the Church of England has never stopped arguing the Reformation. The Elizabethan settlement had cunningly brought supporters of both sides within one portmanteau Church, bundling up the biblical witness of the reformers with Romanist forms of service and church government. Yet reformers and Romanists, low churchmen and high, went on demanding that their side should win; and at the centre of contention was the power of the parson himself. Was he the lord of his flock or not? It is on that still-disputed topic that the lessons of the story chiefly bear.

Work on the book, in the intervals of ordinary journalistic duties, made slow progress until two things happened in 1978 to speed it. The first, in early June, was that Barnes parish church was gutted by fire. The medieval tower and aisle survived, but restoration and rebuilding looked like costing half a million pounds. Clearly a book which heightened the value set on the church in people's minds, locally and nationally, could be helpful; and it might even raise a little money itself. (All royalties from this book go to the Barnes Parish Church Rebuilding Fund.)

The second accelerator, in late November, was the shutdown of Times Newspapers, including the *Sunday Times*. The bulk of the book was written in the ensuing three months. It was an opportunity I would rather not have had, and yet given it I could not but take it.

Barnes, April 1979   John Whale

1 'Inhuman cruelties' (1635-1689)

THE CHURCH AT BARNES GOES BACK WELL BEFORE THE Reformation. The south aisle of the building itself, with the tower at its west end and probably the huge yew near the door as well, dates from the fifteenth century; and at the east end are three lancet windows which belong in style to the thirteenth. Ancient local tradition says the building was consecrated by Archbishop Stephen Langton of Canterbury on his river journey back to Lambeth from the signing of Magna Carta at Runnymede in 1215. The names of incumbents are known even earlier: the first of them was sent out from St Paul's Cathedral in 1199. The dean and chapter endowed the living and remained its patrons. That connection goes a long way to explain the flow of able men and of money to pay them. By the early seventeenth century, when ninety per cent of the parish clergy was paid less than £26 a year, the living of Barnes was worth £140.

Until then the incumbents remain little more than names. We know that the youngish rector installed at Armada time, William Rogers, was put in by Sir Francis Walsingham, Elizabeth I's secretary of state. He lived in Barnes, and had for the time being the appointing of the rectors. So Rogers will have inclined to the reformed or Puritan side, as Walsingham did himself. The same deduction might be made about Thomas Jones, who came in 1614: north Wales and Jesus, Oxford, does not sound a particularly high-church background. (The only other thing known about Jones is that in one period of twelve years at Barnes his wife bore him eight children, and six of them died. The parish's flat terrain, largely enclosed in its omega-shaped river bend, remained pestiferous till it was properly sewered at the end of the nineteenth century.)

John Cutts, though, who followed him, was a clear high-church royalist. It is true that he was 'nursed upon the self-same hill' as Milton: he was at Christ's, Cambridge, with him; but Milton's politics did not rub off on him. His family were old Essex landowners, and his first church was on the family estate. At Barnes he seems to have had some knowledge of his flock: in the burial register he entered 'Ellen Bennet, grandchild to Old Bennet the carrot man'. But when he wrote his will, the object for which he left money was not the poor of the parish but the repair of the church's chancel. It was a high-church interest: it promoted the mysteries which surrounded the priesthood.

Cutts's appointment, in 1635, coincided with a significant movement within the Church of England to the right. Elizabeth I's archbishops of Canterbury (Matthew Parker, Edmund Grindal, John Whitgift) had been reformers. But James I's Richard Bancroft was a man of more conservative mind. Scholars like Richard Hooker, Bishop Lancelot Andrewes and John Donne, dean of St Paul's in the 1620s, held a high doctrine of the Church and the priesthood to match the high Stuart doctrine of the Crown. Priests as well as kings were indelibly ordained of God. The clinching appointment was of William Laud to Canterbury in 1633, under Charles I. Laud and his friends were for episcopacy, ordered ritual, and cruel discipline in enforcing them. Puritans saw all that as the advance of popery: they mistrusted it as much as Charles's claims for the monarchy. That was part of the division which produced the Civil War; and it was a part which the Civil War did not settle.

So the king gathered his forces; and when he made his war headquarters at Oxford in the autumn of 1642, the rector of Barnes was in his company. (Cutts may not have had much choice: the parliamentary army was encamped just down-stream of Barnes at Putney, and as a known royalist Cutts may not have felt safe in his own parish.) Parliament – the Long Parliament – declared the living vacant. Over the next few years a couple of thousand incumbents were similarly turned

out elsewhere. There were twenty-three of them among Cutts's
own friends: to them, too, he left money. He died soon enough
for it to be useful in relieving distress.

The Church was now run from Parliament. Two rival groups
from Barnes went there in 1643 to ask for a new rector. The
king's men went to the Lords to make the case for a local
royalist. The Parliament men went to the Commons: the new
MPs were mostly Presbyterians, believers in a measure of local
church autonomy. This second delegation wanted Thomas
Rutton, an active Presbyterian who had been taking the
services during Cutts's absence. Eight or ten years earlier he had
left Emmanuel, the most Puritan of colleges at either university.
Rutton got the job. Eight months later he was made rector of
St Mary le Bow, in the City, as well. (Pluralism persisted in all
parts of the Church of England late into the nineteenth
century.) He forfeited that job when the wind changed again at
the Restoration; but Barnes he lost sooner than that, in 1647.
He gave way to a man with better connections than his own:
Robert Lenthall.

Lenthall was second cousin to the Speaker of the Long
Parliament, William Lenthall – the man who had resisted
Charles I's attempt to arrest five members five years before, and
who became a close associate of Cromwell's. Robert Lenthall's
transfer to Barnes seems to have been a matter of compassion as
much as connections; and he was the kind of man who attracted
it. He had been rector of Great Hampden in Buckinghamshire;
and within a space of six weeks there, in August and September
1647, he had lost five members of his household to 'the sickness'
– one of the outbreaks of unidentified plague which periodically
visited the home counties. First his only daughter died, then his
wife, then a small boy living in the house, then his only son,
then a boy cousin. Lenthall himself entered their deaths in the
Great Hampden parish register. His twenty-one-year-old son
Adrian he described as 'a hopeful young man'; but the death
which clearly affected him most was that of his daughter Sarah,
who was at home only on a brief visit, and whose end he
recorded with a touching exactitude, as if the accumulation of
detail could keep her with him a little longer. 'My daughter

Sarah Lenthall was buried the eleventh day of August', he wrote. 'She came from London to Wycombe on the Saturday only to see us and so to return the morrow in the afternoon to Wycombe again, but then fell sick, and on Wednesday morning following (being the eleventh of August) about an hour before sunrise died of the sickness; and so in the evening we buried her in the mead called the kitchenmead by the hedge side as you go down into it on your left hand, a little below the pond at the entrance into the mead. She was aged fourteen years eleven months and seventeen days; had she lived to Bartholomew day she had been full fifteen years of age.'

Barnes brought him a little comfort. He married again, and lived another eleven years. By a pleasing irony, this gentle man left a clearer mark on the place than many of his more forceful successors. In 1652 he planted four elms and three ash trees, with his own hand, in the churchyard (chronicling the deed in the same discursive style in the register). The trees lived far longer than he can have expected. Two survived into the twentieth century; the last of them fell victim to Dutch elm disease in 1977.

Lenthall was briefly succeeded at his death in 1658 by one Griffith. There was a Puritan divine of the same name who came from Montgomeryshire in mid-Wales, was an undergraduate at Magdalen, Oxford, was presumably uneasy at that high-church college, transferred to Emmanuel, Cambridge, and was made a fellow of Trinity, Cambridge (by Parliament) in 1646. He was a Congregationalist – like Cromwell himself, and Milton: theirs was the other main sect, besides the Presbyterians, to which the Puritans belonged. If this was indeed the Griffith who is known to have been appointed to Barnes, he was in any case so busy as a leader of Congregationalism in London that he had no time for his appointed cure of souls. His name never once appears in the parish register; it was kept instead by one Thomas Snignall, with the entries comparatively few and ill-written.

All these men, the Ruttons and the Griffiths and the subordinate Snignalls, were engulfed by the Restoration. Even if it followed chiefly from the unpopularity and disunity of the army, it had profound ecclesiastical consequences which could not have come about unless Puritan churchmen had grown to be as much disliked as Puritan soldiers. Bishops emerged from prison. Cathedrals, which had been used as barracks or prisoner-of-war cages by both sides, became places of worship again. The dean and chapter of St Paul's reasserted the right of appointment to the living of Barnes. Charles II entered London at the end of May 1660: the new rector was in his functions by August.

His name was John Squire. He was not himself one of the high-churchmen thrown out in the early 1640s: he was finishing his education at Jesus, Oxford, at the time; but his father had been. The son's most visible achievement was to marry a woman of intellect. He died young, after he had been rector little more than a year; but his wife put up to his memory a large oval tablet which stood for more than three centuries as the best written in Barnes church, balanced in thought and phrase. A prefatory Latin pun identified it as a tribute to a deserving husband from a sorrowing wife:

'*Merentissimo conjugi conjux maerentissima.* To the best of husbands John Squire, the late faithful and (oh that for so short a time) painful rector of this parish – the only son to that most strenuous propugnator of piety and loyalty (both by preaching and suffering) John Squire, sometime vicar of St Leonard's, Shoreditch, near London – Grace Lynch (who bare unto him one only daughter) consecrated this (such as it is) small monument of their mutual affection. He was invested in this care in 1660, on September 2; he was divested of all care in 1662, on January 9, aged 42 years.'

('Painful', of course, in the sense of taking pains.)

The living of Barnes was then bestowed on one of the most notorious of those 1640s sufferers: Dr Edward Layfield. As a nephew of Archbishop Laud, Layfield had risen fast. In 1633, not long out of St John's, Oxford (his uncle's college), he was given a prebend – a non-residentiary but paid canonry – at St Paul's; the next year he collected the archdeaconry of Essex as well; and the year after that he also became vicar of All Hallows,

Barking (since called All Hallows by the Tower). Layfield was
zealous in his anti-Puritanism, and known for it. The Puritans
in his congregation at All Hallows complained. When the Long
Parliament met in 1640, among its first acts were to have Laud
arrested (he was later executed) and his nephew's forms of
worship examined. Findings in the Layfield case were recorded
in the Commons journals in illuminating detail.

The chief cause of offence was the way he took the communion
service. 'He hath set up the communion table altarwise, and
caused rails and ten several images upon those rails to be set at
the altar.' These were little wooden statues of saints. Layfield
also 'said to the people "Heretofore we see Christ by faith, but
now with our fleshly eyes we see him in the sacrament." When
these images were taken down he charged them with sacrilege.
He refused to give the sacrament to his people unless they came
to the altar, though they had offered reverently kneeling to
receive the same in the body of the church. He caused one
Boulton to be excommunicated for not coming up to the rails to
receive, and refused to read his absolution. He said he would not
for a hundred pounds come from the rails to give the sacrament;
nay, he would rather lose his living.'

What made all this offensive to Puritans and reformers was
their rediscovery, in the Bible, of the assurance that man is
saved by grace and faith alone. He cannot earn his salvation,
and does not need to: it has been won for him, once for all, by
Christ. The believing sinner needs no other mediator before
God – neither saint (hence the reformers' hostility to images)
nor priest (which partly explained their dislike of deference to
clerics). Nor does Christ's mediating act need ever to be done
again; and that was why the reformers rejected any claim that
the communion bread and wine became Christ's body and
blood, and could be offered anew, at an altar demanding
special reverence, in the sacrifice of the Mass.

The Commons ordered Layfield and his curate at All Hallows
to allow certain approved divines (not necessarily in orders) to
preach before the parishioners, so that they might choose a
'lecturer'. Here was congregationalism indeed. The Puritans
among the parishioners made a choice and gave the Commons

the name. The Commons declared Layfield deprived as a delinquent, and unfit to hold any church post. Layfield refused to obey the order of deprivation without trial. He was dragged from the church while he was taking a service, set on a horse, and forced to ride to prison with his surplice tied behind him and the Prayer Book hung round his neck. He also lost livings at Wrotham in Kent and Chiddingfold in Surrey: his wife, who with his nine children was till then amply provided for, was reduced to applying to a committee of Parliament sitting at Kingston-upon-Thames for a one-fifth share of the Chiddingfold income. There is no sign that she got it. Layfield himself saw the inside of most of the gaols in London, and was at one time held in a prison-ship on the Thames under threat of being transported overseas.

But he was a doughty survivor. He survived his spell in the wilderness. Restored to All Hallows the year after he succeeded Squire at Barnes, he survived the Great Plague. It was at its worst in London in the middle 1660s; and there was not much added safety at Barnes, where several people died of it. (Charles II's court retreated from Hampton Court to Salisbury.) He survived the next scourge, the Great Fire, which destroyed old St Paul's and many other church buildings: he rebuilt the parsonage house at All Hallows and lived in it for the rest of his life. He survived his wife, burying her there in 1678; and held on to his functions as rector of Barnes, a cheerful absentee, until his own death in 1680.

Yet the Church was not made up of Layfields. His successor, Hezekiah Burton, was a man of a significantly different stamp. He was one of a group of churchmen who grappled with a problem which troubled Layfield not at all: that the post-Restoration ejections would prolong quarrelling, not end it.

The number of clergymen put out with Griffith in 1660 was about seven hundred. Charles II still showed signs of wanting an accommodation with the Puritans; but MPs gave him little help. In 1661 the Anglicans produced a new Prayer Book; and none of its changes was in a Puritan direction. It said, for example, with very little qualification, that people taking communion were to be 'all meekly kneeling'. Parliament

approved the book in the early months of 1662, and pinned it
to an Act of Uniformity which made it the only legal service-
book. The Act became law on May 19; by August 24, St
Bartholomew's day, every minister was to adopt it or resign. To
turn the screw, those of them who had been ordained by elders
of their own churches were to have themselves reordained by
bishops.

It was the final blow. There were more than a thousand
'Bartholomeans' or nonconformists who could not accept it,
though all self-interest ran the other way. And not content with
compelling the Puritans to leave the Church, Parliament
punished them for being outside it. A series of Acts forbad them
to take municipal office or meet for worship.

The attempt to end dissenting opinions by outlawing them
produced its ordinary result, which was to give them new
strength. Parliament argued that it was hemmed in. It could
not indulge Puritans without also accommodating Roman
Catholics (who suffered from the same restraints); and that
would revive the old threat of their growing strong enough to
bring in foreign help. The century before, that had been on
offer from Spain. Now it might be had from France. Louis
XIV was a fervent Roman Catholic with a very high doctrine
of kingship indeed. Puritans would abolish the monarchy;
Roman Catholics would turn it into a tyranny.

Hezekiah Burton, the rector of Barnes who addressed this
difficulty, came from a Nottinghamshire family of modest
means and Puritan leanings. (His father's name, too, was
Hezekiah: the Puritans liked scriptural names.) He was a clever
child: he went up to Magdalene, Cambridge, at the age of
fifteen. He did well enough there to be a fellow by the time he
was twenty-two, in 1654; and he stayed for another nine years
as a tutor, becoming a well-known Cambridge figure. He was
commemorated in a portrait painted by Mary Beale, a protégée
of Lely's. (Charles II was another of her sitters.) The painting
hangs in the college parlour still, looking out across First Court
to russet-brick walls which are much as they were in Burton's
time, having been stuccoed and unstuccoed in the interval. In
the picture, his dark hair reaches almost to the shoulders of his

Hezekiah Burton

sober clerical suit; and his face has the clear-eyed tranquillity of a man who feels sure enough of what he himself believes to be unaffronted by the knowledge that there are other people who believe something slightly different.

Samuel Pepys, diarist and civil servant, had been up at Magdalene a few years before: the two man knew each other. But the college connection which proved most important to Burton was with Sir Orlando Bridgman, a lawyer-politician. Burton took orders in 1661, and two years later left Magdalene to become a Northamptonshire vicar. In 1667 Bridgman succeeded Clarendon as one of Charles II's chief ministers (in the office of Lord Keeper of the Great Seal). He made Burton his chaplain, and found him a Norwich Cathedral post whose duties were not burdensome. As a result, Burton was able to live at Bridgman's rooms in London; they were at Essex House, beside the Temple.

Here Burton gathered congenial churchmen. Among his friends were John Tillotson, later dean and then archbishop of Canterbury; Edward Stillingfleet, later dean of St Paul's and then bishop of Worcester; and John Wilkins, master of Trinity, Cambridge, and later bishop of Chester. These men were called by the religious world, sometimes dismissively, latitudinarians: that is to say, they believed that the Christian faith could be expressed in certain broad, scriptural principles, within which diversities of belief could be allowed a good deal of latitude. It was a creed which exalted good sense above zeal; and its time seemed to have come. In August 1667, when Bridgman came to office, the capital had barely recovered from the successive devastations of plague and fire, and French conquests in the Netherlands had heightened the apparent risk of foreign Catholic intervention. It was no time for Protestants to be divided. Bridgman certainly thought so. In January 1668 he set up serious and secret negotiations intended to draw at least the Presbyterians back into the Anglican fold. (The Congregationalists had already decided that they must remain outside it.) The negotiators for the Presbyterians were Richard Baxter, their saintly leader, and William Bates; for the Anglicans, Wilkins and Burton.

As Bridgman's chaplain, Burton was the natural link between churchmen and statesmen of a conciliatory turn. He was also fitted for the job by temperament. He left behind two volumes of sermons, which Tillotson edited; and they well express, in the sinewy and dateless prose of the time, Burton's instinctive tolerance. He starts from the necessity of religion: 'No man that is not religious can be either acceptable to God or pleasing to himself; and no man can be happy without both these.' And his hearers are not to suppose that any religion will do. 'As it's necessary man should be of some, it's no less necessary he should be of the true religion. A false religion may be of as little avail, nay, perhaps more prejudicial to him that's of it, than none at all. The least that can be said of it is that it's labour lost, that a man takes pains to no purpose: he travels in a way that will never bring him to heaven.'

But the test of whether a religion was true or not was in its fruits. 'The sum is, that religion obliges us to all that's good, and nothing else', Burton argued. 'Some have entertained such an opinion of it, as if it made men worse than without it they would be; and I wish there were not too much ground for this calumny. For 'tis too true that the religion of some men hath made them not only affectedly singular, morose and humoursome; less affable, and more conceited of themselves, censuring and despising others; but hath engaged them likewise to lying and falseness, to bloody massacres and inhuman cruelties towards those that but differed from them in some trifling opinions.' None of that, though, came from true religion. 'Let these and all that by such mistakes render religion so odious know that to be religious and to do good are the same thing: they that think otherwise, they know not what religion is.'

He returned more than once to that theme, as a mediator's rebuke to the extremists on both sides. 'Let no man think the worse of religion for the mischief which they do who are pretenders to it. And when he sees states overturned, countries laid waste, the blood of thousands spilled; honest, harmless, virtuous men who fear God, imitate their Saviour and love all men – when he sees such as these imprisoned, dungeoned, tortured, and at last perhaps burnt at a stake; let him not then say, this is religion; no, but this is irreligion; this is from profaneness, from ignorance or hatred of God that these things are done.' And he concluded: 'As soon may the sun bring forth darkness as the religion of Christ this.'

Baxter, for his part, was more disposed to compromise than seven years before by his knowledge of the sufferings of nonconformist ministers. They had to travel great distances at night to minister to their charges; and yet most of them continued to minister, just as they had during the Plague, when they had ventured into parts of London which Anglican clerics had deserted. In this worsened atmosphere the basis of the proposals put forward by Wilkins and Burton was that Presbyterian ministers should be ordained by bishops, to make their orders acceptable within the Church of England; that they should declare their approval of the 'doctrine, worship and government established in the Church of England, as containing all things necessary to salvation'; and that various points in the Prayer Book like kneeling at communion should be 'left indifferent, or taken away'. By this means Presbyterians would be 'comprehended' – reabsorbed into the Church of England. Congregationalists, meanwhile, were to be 'indulged' – allowed to meet for public worship, but still 'disabled from bearing any public office'.

Baxter was worried that the declaration required to bring Presbyterians in might not be stringent enough to keep Roman Catholics out. In the end, though, that was not the problem. 'The grand stop in our treaty', Baxter later remembered, 'was about reordination.' Wilkins was insistent: 'those consciences must be accommodated who took them for no ministers who were ordained without bishops.' Baxter saw the grave slight that this would be on all Protestant nonconformists, and counterproposed a form of words which would show that reordination was a legal, not a theological, requirement. It even seemed possible that his proposal would succeed; and he believed that the whole deal would have been joyfully accepted by some fourteen hundred, or about two-thirds, of 'the nonconformable ministers of England'.

But at that moment word of the negotiations came to the ears of Clarendon's old friends in Parliament. 'Alas!' Baxter wrote, 'all this labour was in vain: for the active prelates and prelatists so far prevailed that as soon as ever the Parliament met, without any delay, they took notice that there was a rumour abroad of some motions or Act to be offered for comprehension or indulgence; and voted, that no man should bring in such an Act into the House. And so they prevented all talk or motion of such a thing; and the Lord Keeper, that had called us and set us on work, himself turned that way, and talked after as if he understood us not.'

Burton, too, seems to have been disillusioned by the experience. He left Bridgman's service, and took no part in a similarly unsuccessful venture six years later. Instead he plunged back into the parish ministry. He became rector (on Bridgman's gift) of St George's, Southwark. Tillotson, bringing out Burton's sermons after his death, prefaced them with an affectionate memoir in which he recorded Burton's twelve Southwark years in these terms: 'Besides his constant pains in preaching and catechizing, he employed a great part of his time in offices and acts of charity, in visitation of the sick, and a most tender and compassionate care of the poor, which in that parish were exceeding many, besides the two great prisons of the King's Bench and Marshalsea, which he often visited, and bestowed there not only his own charity but all that by his interest and solicitation he could obtain from others; by which means he not only continually relieved but every year released a very considerable number of poor prisoners for small debts, to the great comfort of many poor families. This, together with his exemplary conversation among them in all humility and kindness and meekness of wisdom, made him to be exceedingly beloved in his parish during his continuance with them, and his departure from them to be greatly lamented.'

Burton did not by disposition find those years easy; but the tolerance born of humankindness helped him. He spoke in his last major sermon (which may well have been preached at Barnes as he looked back over his Southwark years) of the 'extraordinary diligence' which ministers must deploy 'to carry them through all the opposition and difficulties they shall

certainly meet with in their general converse with all sorts –
with men of the meanest capacities, of lowest rank, and greatest
vices, and worst natures. Nothing but this universal benevolence
can fit them for such converse: only he that loves all will bear
with such conversation as a minister meets with.'

Yet his instinct in going back to parish life had been right.
There was now nothing left to try towards preventing a formal
split within English Protestantism. It seemed likely to come in
1672, when the king – acting on his own initiative – issued a
declaration of indulgence which recognized both Protestant nonconformists and Roman Catholics. Each group was to be allowed
to worship in its separate way. Over fourteen hundred nonconformist ministers exercised their new right to be licensed as such.

But Parliament did not yet realize that these men could not
be coerced. It forced the king to withdraw his indulgence, and
in 1673 strengthened the Clarendon Code with a Test Act
which laid a new requirement on people in public offices: they
must show their Anglicanism by taking communion according
to the Anglican rite – an invitation to cynical conformism
which remained in force till 1828. In the words of Cowper's
poem *Expostulation*, the Act 'made the symbols of atoning grace
An office-key, a pick-lock to a place'.

It was not as if these differences in religious belief could any
longer be thought likely to disappear. They persisted within
Anglicanism itself. That is well enough shown by the difficulty
which marked the process whereby Burton, towards the end of
his life, was appointed to Barnes. When Layfield finally passed
to his reward in 1680, three names were put forward for the
succession; and they corresponded to three distinct strands
within the Church of England. One was Layfield's son-in-law,
Francis Hawkins, chaplain to the Tower of London: he represented the old high-church faction. One was Richard Kidder,
who had been a fellow of Emmanuel and a Bartholomean before
he came back to the fold: he stood for the low-church, Puritan
interest. The third was Burton, the broad-churchman. Burton
had the backing of Tillotson, who was dean of Canterbury at
the time; and since the dean of St Paul's was Stillingfleet,
another old friend, Burton's claim prevailed.

Both his defeated rivals went on to deaneries; Burton never had the chance. Less than a year later, at the age of forty-nine, he was carried off by a Barnes fever. A son of his died three days later; and there seem to have been other deaths in the household. Tillotson – in sentences which show why Dryden acknowledged a debt to him as a prose stylist – wrote Burton's obituary thus:

'For about a year before his death he was removed to Barnes, not far from London; where he was seized upon by a very dangerous and malignant fever, of which he died, and several of his family.

'It pleased the wise providence of God, whose ways are not as our ways, nor his thoughts as our thoughts, to take this good man from us in the ripeness of his age, when he was capable of doing the greatest service to the Church of God, and in a time when he was most likely to have contributed considerably to it, as being by the incomparable sweetness of his temper and prudence of his behaviour admirably fitted to allay those heats which then began to break out, but are since blown up to all the degrees of a violent and implacable enmity by the skill and industry of a crafty and restless party among us, playing upon our weakness, and persuading us to receive odious names of distinction and to fling them like squibs and fireballs at one another, to make the Philistines sport; so that we have great reason to lament the loss of so useful a man in so needful a time.

'I shall only mention those good qualities and virtues which were more remarkable in him: his great piety towards God, the native simplicity of his mind and manners, the singular kindness of his conversation, and his cheerful readiness to every good work; but above all the sincerity of his friendship, for I never knew any man that upon all occasions served his friend with that forwardness and zeal and unwearied diligence as he would do, and with less consideration of himself and his own interest. He was infinitely troubled to see the abounding of iniquity and the abatement of charity among us, but he did not live to see the worst of it, and to what a height our senseless heats and animosities are since risen. God was pleased to take him away from that unpleasant sight, which would certainly have been as grievous to him as to any man living.'

One of the closing sentences in Burton's last sermon puts the message of his life even more succinctly. 'If heaven be more desirable than hell, it's better to love than to hate.' It was a plea which met with only indirect success. James II, succeeding his brother in 1685, destroyed himself by his zeal to help Roman Catholics; and his replacement at the end of 1688, William III, was a Dutch Calvinist who could hardly be expected to support the continued outlawry of Calvin's followers in England. Even the king's advocacy could not make Parliament and the Church accept ideas of the Burton stamp, still in circulation, for adjusting the Prayer Book to accommodate Protestant non-conformists. But a Toleration Act the following year provided that, although they would still be debarred from public office and the universities, they might broadly worship as they liked. Although it was not an acceptance of Burton's message, it was at least a recognition of reality.

2 'The blessings we enjoy' (1688-1749)

THE BELLS WERE BUSY IN THE BRICK TOWER OF BARNES church as the seventeenth century gave way to the eighteenth. They had the Glorious Revolution of 1688 to ring in, when James was replaced by William III and Mary. They marked Queen Anne's proclamation and coronation in 1702. They signalled every favourable turn in the European balance-of-power struggle, with the English and the French on opposite sides, which filled her reign: the War of the Spanish Succession. The occasions were noted in the vestry-book: 'when Barcelona was taken . . . victory in Brabant . . . Admiral Lake burnt the ships . . . Prince Eugene beat the French . . . Milan was taken . . . Prince Eugene and duke of Savoy raised the siege . . . Prince Eugene and duke of Savoy beat the French . . .'

It was too much to hope that, with the dissenters gone, the struggle was over within Anglicanism. There were still upholders of conscience as against authority left within the fold. The same split was coming into view in politics: the labels Whig and Tory were already in use. Certainly, with its left thinned out, the Church of England inclined to the right. The tendency was most marked under Anne. She was James's second surviving child; and although, like her elder sister Mary, she was brought up an Anglican, within that persuasion she remained a high-churchwoman and a Tory. Under her the Church grew in missionary confidence. New churches were built, old ones restored. The new St Paul's itself was topped out during her reign: in 1710, at the age of seventy-seven, Sir Christopher Wren was hoisted up to see his son lay the highest stone of the lantern on top of the dome.

The rector throughout this time was William Richardson. He followed Burton in 1681, and stayed at Barnes till his own death in 1717. (He was there long enough to have Handel as a parishioner for a year at the end.) Like Burton, he was a young man of plain origins from the east Midlands who became a Cambridge don. He came from Stamford in Lincolnshire: his college at Cambridge was Clare, where he was a sizar, as Burton had been at Magdalene. Sizars had financial help from their colleges, and at that time a certain amount of sweeping and bed-making and water-carrying to do in exchange.

Barnes was still in effect a country parish, with fewer than two hundred inhabitants, and a great deal of open ground occasionally holed for supplies of turf and sand (the source of the income from which the churchwardens paid the bell-ringers and renewed the ropes). It was the country clergy in particular who were Tory high-churchmen – men not marked out by any great difference in wealth or social standing from most of their flock, and therefore needing all the more to make much of their priestly dignity. William Richardson, the sizar from Stamford, might have been expected to be of their party.

But the most significant fact about Richardson is his marriage. It showed that his links were with another kind of church-manship. In 1678, the year after he took his M.A. he became a fellow of his college. By the end of 1681 he was rector of Barnes; and in the summer of 1682 he married. Oxford and Cambridge dons could not marry and keep their fellowships; so the wedding was either the reason for his leaving Clare or the consequence of it. He and his wife had five children in the next seven years.

She was Mary Stillingfleet, a niece of Edward Stillingfleet: he was still dean of St Paul's. So it was Stillingfleet who arranged and approved the appointment of a man who was anyway his niece's intended husband. The double bond presupposes that Richardson shared Stillingfleet's peaceable outlook.

More than that, the appointment was in a literal sense a piece of nepotism – the giving of good jobs by great men to their own nephews. It was barely a year since Stillingfleet had done the same favour to his old friend Burton. And the dean was one of

the most admired divines of his time. He would have defended
the practice by saying that these were men whom he knew to be
sound. But it gave countenance to other men of power who
appointed their friends and relations on no better ground than
that they were friends or relations; and it fostered an atmosphere
in which both the bestowers and the holders of church posts
could regard them as merely a source of income. A living was a
living and nothing more.

It was in the first half of the eighteenth century that the
Church of England most clearly exhibited that cool and worldly
quality which it has been a long time losing. The point is as well
illustrated in Barnes as anywhere. The next four rectors after
Richardson were all members of the St Paul's chapter, which
means that they were happy to see its patronage used not just
for their friends' benefit but for their own; they were all
pluralists; at least three of them were manifestly interested in
money; two of them became bishops, and held on to other posts
after they had been thus elevated. Of them all, the ablest and
most open worldling was Richardson's immediate successor,
Francis Hare – a political prelate who came within a touch of
the archbishopric of Canterbury.

The prime exhibit for the understanding of Hare's character
and career is a huge lump of white marble. It stands in a side-
chapel of King's College chapel at Cambridge, unsubmerged by
the sea of stacked and folded chairs which now habitually
surrounds it, surmounted by a funerary urn, and with painted
red-and-gold flames coming out of the top. It is a cenotaph for a
King's undergraduate who died of smallpox in 1702. His
epitaph covers both flanks of the monument. On the side nearer
the door are set out in Latin his name, his parentage, a handful
of superlatives about his unsurpassed gifts, and an intimation
that details are to be found on the further side. There the reader
discovers three hundred closely-carved words of the most
elegant Latinity imaginable, full of choice tropes and Ciceronian
rhythms, ascribing to the young man in so many words every
virtue of body and mind. It is something of a surprise to reach
the bottom line and discover that the paragon who had given
proof of so many qualities was a boy of sixteen. The matter,

inevitably, is thin: the poor child was friendly, went to chapel
twice a day and turned up for classes on time; but the manner is
superb.

The dead boy was the marquis of Blandford. His father was
duke of Marlborough. The obituarist, a don at King's at the
time, was Francis Hare.

Hare was a man of wide reading in Greek and Hebrew as well
as Latin, bustling energy, and a total grasp of the Church of
England's current doctrinal and political problems. He used all
his abilities to serve a single end; his own advancement. He had
come to King's from a landed family in Essex, by way of Eton.
At Cambridge he chose his pupils perspicaciously: another of
them was Robert Walpole, a son of the leading Whig landowner
in Norfolk and a precious connection thirty years on. But the
foundation of Hare's fortunes was the Blandford tomb. The
reader whose heart it chiefly touched, as it must have been
designed to do, was the boy's father.

Marlborough was Anne's captain-general, and commander-
in-chief of a force of English, Dutch and German soldiers
fighting the French across Europe. (The principal theatre of
war was Belgium and northern France – the same region fought
over in another bitter balance-of-power conflict two centuries
later, in which some of the same place-names recurred: the
First World War.) The captain-general needed a chaplain-
general. He hired Hare.

Hare was neither cowardly nor idle. He was present at the
battles of Blenheim (in 1704, beside the Danube) and Ramillies
(in 1706, near the Meuse). He was close enough to the action to
write useful accounts of it in letters to a cousin. He seems to have
accompanied Marlborough through eight campaigning summers;
and he was not the man to lose an opportunity of digging
himself yet deeper into the graces of the great. A thanksgiving
sermon he preached to the Commons at St Margaret's,
Westminster, was a fair specimen of his method. The sermon was
delivered early in 1709, the winter after Marlborough's third
big victory, Oudenarde. It sounded much more like a war
correspondent's glorification of the duke than a minister's
homage to God, and was rescued only by rare and perfunctory

scriptural allusions. 'After a continued march of two nights and
two days – for so I call a march interrupted only by the halt of a
few hours, which was more for a blind to the enemy than
refreshment to the troops – on the third day the army marched
again, passed in the face of the enemy a large and rapid river,
beat them from the strongest posts with scarce half their
number, and after a great slaughter forced them to a most
ignominious retreat; and all this in less time than the bare
disposition for a battle in such ground, according to the rules of
war, could have been made. With such rapidity did these
heroes run to victory, "They were swifter than eagles, they were
stronger than lions." ' Hare went on in the same vein for the
best part of an hour.

In September 1711 he preached at Avesnes-le-Sec, near
Arras, with Marlborough in the congregation. The duke had
just won his last success, the capture of Bouchain. Hare cut his
running-time to half an hour, and compared the great man to
Joshua and Moses. The notable lack in the sermon is any sense
of the misery of war, even though Marlborough's campaigns had
afforded plenty of instances. (The sense survives even in
Thackeray's *Esmond*, written about the war a hundred and
forty years later. Hare himself wins the honour of a mention –
as having been Blandford's moral tutor – in the most magical
sequence in the book, where Esmond comes home at Christmas
from his own first campaign in 1702, and is reconciled to his
mentor Lady Castlewood.) Hare, from his French pulpit,
encouraged the duke to press on. 'Can we think it reasonable
to give out before we have attained our end?' he asked. 'The
true use we ought to make of the successes we are blessed
with is to take courage from them, and "to be strong in the
Lord".'

Hare was in fact answering the general criticism of the war
current in London among opponents of Marlborough and
Walpole (who had for a while been secretary at war). The
principal pamphleteer on the anti-war side was Jonathan Swift.
He had a hand in a direct answer to the Bouchain sermon. 'If a
colonel had been to preach at the head of his regiment, I believe
he would have made just such a sermon', the pamphlet ran.

'What necessity was there of preaching up war to an army who daily enrich themselves by the continuation of it?'

Swift knew Hare's work already. The year before, in his weekly paper the *Examiner*, Swift had made plain his view that Marlborough was continuing the war out of ambition and greed. The most diligent of the writers who replied on Marlborough's behalf – the 'answer-jobbers', Swift called them – was Hare. He produced three pamphlets which Swift described as 'written with some plausibility, much artifice and abundance of misrepresentation'. The temperature of the exchanges rose. In a hasty addition as the last of the three went to press, Hare wrote: 'The *Examiner* is extremely mistaken if he thinks I shall enter the lists with so prostitute a writer, who can neither speak truth nor knows when he hears it. I shall not be moved with the ignorance and malice of a mercenary scribbler, who treats the duke of Marlborough with so much insolence.'

Swift replied in kind. 'The postscript to his third pamphlet was enough to disgust me from having any dealings at all with such a writer; unless that part was left to some footman he had picked up among the boys who follow the camp, whose character it would suit much better than that of the supposed author.' Swift's main contention, developed in another pair of pamphlets during 1712, was that the war was an expensive way of achieving nothing. Nonsense, Hare replied in two further answers: it secured the Protestant succession in Spain's European empire, and checked the power of Catholic France.

Of Hare's last effort, Swift's judgment was that 'the whole is interlarded with a thousand injurious epithets and appellations, which heavy writers are forced to make use of, as a supply for that want of spirit and genius they are not born to'. The comment was just. Hare was out of his class. More than that, he had picked the wrong side, not just to the modern eye but in terms of contemporary politics. The duke lost his command, Bouchain fell again, and England made peace at Utrecht.

Hare had already secured his retreat. Six years earlier, either through Marlborough's influence or Walpole's, he had become a canon of St Paul's (in which dignity he had been one of the commissioners for the new cathedral who had treated the ageing

Wren insufferably, taking the painting of the cupola out of his hands and stopping half his salary on the plea that he was being slow to finish the work). Hare had another security besides: a wealthy wife. He was not a good-looking man; but as well as the favours of the great, he knew how to thrust his way into the regard of rich women. He twice married heiresses. The first, strictly speaking, was an heiress's aunt. After the 1709 campaign he married his first cousin, Bethaia Naylor. Her brother owned Hurstmonceaux Castle in Sussex; and the brother's only child was a three-year-old girl called Grace, said by family tradition to have been the idol of her father's tenants. Two years later the brother and his wife died within a few months of each other. The Hares found themselves Grace's guardians. They moved to the castle from their canonry near St Paul's. A few years later, Bethaia Hare died. Finally the niece herself died, unmarried, at the age of twenty. The belief preserved in the family was that she had been starved to death in one of the castle towers by a jealous governess. Hare will not necessarily have countenanced it, and even the governess may be wrongfully accused: fierce slimming, self-imposed, cannot be a twentieth-century invention. Still, the succession of deaths delivered the castle and its estates first into Hare's control and then into his ownership.

He derived no special satisfaction from them: his letters complain of the expense bequeathed to him by Grace's parents' open-handedness – the deer-park from which 'half the county expected to be supplied with venison', the butts of beer left at the park gates for the refreshment of passers-by, the platoon of old women retained to do nothing but weed the courtyards, the four functionaries whose only duty was to wind the clocks. But the house had the gloomy spaciousness of the late middle ages; and his possession of it did at least mean that when Hare became rector of Barnes in 1717 he had somewhere else to live while the humble parsonage there was being refashioned to his taste.

Hare's second wife, Margaret Alston, was the eldest daughter of an East Anglian landowner whose estates lay near Hare's family property. He married her in 1728, the year after he had resigned the Barnes post. She persuaded him (probably without much difficulty) to pull the castle down and rebuild it as

Hurstmonceaux Place. She tried to wrest the succession away
from the son of Hare's first marriage and bestow it on her own
children by Hare. (There were seven of them. Three died in
infancy.) She was unsuccessful; but the Hares were not in any
case short of places to lay their heads. Besides land in Norfolk
and Suffolk, the second Mrs Hare brought with her a charming
Buckinghamshire house, the Vache at Chalfont St Giles.
Wherever church preferment took him – the deaneries of
Worcester and then St Paul's were his next berths – this now
became Hare's favourite home. But first it too had to be
suitably altered. He hung a fifty-yard gallery with portraits of
his ancestors; he fitted up an old chapel in the grounds for one
of his chaplains to say divine service in. His hand was also felt
in the parish church. It contains to this day a handsome five-
sectioned oak altar-rail, wide and welcoming to the kneeler's
hands above, carved in a leaf-pattern below. Hare provided it
by a simple exercise of his authority as dean of St Paul's: he
removed it from his new cathedral.

He was a man with a sense of fitting dignity and comfort.
Barnes was his only descent into parish work, and a limited one.
His name seldom appears in the parish register: he leant
heavily on curates and churchwardens. (One of his churchwardens in 1720 was Jacob Tonson, the publisher and book-
seller, who founded the Kit Cat club for his literary and
political acquaintance – Walpole became a member – and
moved its meetings in about 1703 to a house he had bought in
Barnes.) All the time Hare was there he also had the castle and a
deanery to live in. He nevertheless insisted that Barnes rectory
itself should be reconstructed. In his first year he won from the
St Paul's chapter, as one of its own number, authorization 'to
fell, cut down and take away so many timber trees of oak or elm
upon the demesnes of the manor of Barnes . . . as you shall have
occasion for towards the repairing or rebuilding of the parsonage
house'. The splendid square-fronted brown-brick house which
still stands beside the church tower, with a giant copper beech
of comparable age on the lawn behind, dates largely from
Hare's time.

He was a classic pluralist. For nearly all his working life he held two jobs, for much of it three, and at one stage four. From 1707 he was supplementing the chaplain-generalcy with his canonry at St Paul's, which he held for the rest of his life. Demobilized, he eked the canonry out with a royal chaplaincy and a seat on the governing body at Eton (jobs which will at the least have earned him a few dinners). In 1715, when Hare was forty-four, his career took off. In that year he collected the deanery of Worcester. Two years later he added the incumbency at Barnes, which gave him (with his canonry) three salaries at once. In 1722 he added a fourth, secular, stipend: he was appointed to the £1000-a-year sinecure of usher to the exchequer by a politician related to his first wife, Henry Pelham. But Pelham left the Treasury Board for the War Office two years later, and Hare will have departed too. In 1726 he repaired his income by moving from Worcester to the richer deanery of St Paul's; he still remained a canon of the same cathedral, and rector of Barnes. He only gave up Barnes (but not the two St Paul's posts) in the following year, when he became bishop of St Asaph in north Wales; he was translated to the more lucrative bishopric of Chichester four years later. He held it from 1731 till his death in 1740. For the last thirteen years of his life, therefore, his three concurrent jobs were a canonry, a deanery and a bishopric. And all this was in addition to the considerable landed wealth which came to him from his father and his wives.

Part of this worldly success arose from the favour Hare found with two women even better placed than his two wives: Queen Anne, and George II's Queen Caroline. Anne was a dim but resolute and patriotic figure to whom Hare's Tory piety made ready appeal. 'If we do our duty to God in our private capacities as men and Christians,' he said in his sermon to the Commons, 'that will naturally lead us to obey him in his vice-gerent, and teach us, as members of a civil state, to discharge with integrity and zeal the duties which he, in whom all government is founded, has laid on us. It will teach us, as a part of thankfulness to God, to love and honour the queen, who deserves of her people all possible marks of duty and affection for her own sake. For it is not her piety and goodness only we are indebted to for

the blessings we enjoy under her. She possesses not only the
female virtues – for so some would have devotion and piety and
goodness called, to excuse their own want of them – but, thanks
be to God, all the other virtues also that are the glory of the
throne and the happiness of the people shine forth eminently
in her.'

The royal chaplaincy which Anne bestowed on Hare in 1712
in consideration of sermons like these was taken away again by
George I six years later, when combative right-wing views were
out of fashion. In the song, the vicar of Bray found it wise to
trim at that point:

> When George in pudding-time came o'er
> And moderate men looked big, Sir,
> My politics I changed once more
> And I became a Whig, Sir.

But Hare was a cut above the vicar of Bray. He simply bided
his time; and when in 1727 the whirligig of time brought in the
robust and undoctrinaire Queen Caroline, whose husband
allowed her the liberty to make bishops in return for his
freedom to keep mistresses, Hare was on the bench of bishops
within months. He did not waste his chances. Lord Hervey's
Memoirs of the Reign of George II show him to have been by 1736
an intimate at court. He and Hervey were rival courtiers, in
fact; the queen relayed to each of them the other's sarcasms
about him.

The other element in Hare's advancement was his link with
Walpole. The bread he had cast on the waters as a young don
at King's was returning to him after many days. The two men
had kept in touch. It was early in 1715 that Walpole became in
effect the Crown's chief minister; and that was the year when
Hare attained his first deanery. Walpole perfectly shared Hare's
view of the uses of office. In about 1730 Hare's eldest son by his
second wife was christened Robert: Walpole stood godfather.
As a christening present the great -man gave his godson a
government post worth £400 a year: the sweepership of
Gravesend. The only duty entailed was to go down to Gravesend
once a year and distribute ten guineas among the town's

watermen. Robert Hare was an apt pupil. Not merely did he
hold on to the sweepership for the rest of his life, but he repeated
his father's feat of marrying two heiresses in succession. (The
first one died of a chill brought on by eating too many ices at a
ball.) He ended his days as a canon of Winchester.

Once Hare was bishop of Chichester, Walpole's influence
almost pushed him further yet. In 1736 Archbishop Wake of
Canterbury was nearly eighty, and dying. Walpole wanted the
job for Hare – as much out of political vanity as friendship,
since Hare was known to have been his tutor, and the appointment would have been a clear sign that the man who ran the
country was Walpole.

But there was a kind of justice even in the affairs of the
eighteenth-century Church. The hard-driving spirit of self-
aggrandisement which had brought Hare so far now stopped
him short of the big prize. The queen was in any case inclined
to favour Bishop Sherlock of Salisbury, whom Walpole disliked;
but Hare was destroyed by his own disposition. Hervey himself
put the point. 'You will certainly repent of it', he told Walpole,
'if you take Hare. He is a haughty, hard-natured, imperious,
hot-headed, injudicious fellow, who, I firmly believe, would
give you more trouble at Lambeth than even Sherlock himself;
and besides that, is so thoroughly disliked in private and feared
in public life that I do not think you could lodge power in more
unpopular hands.' He urged the same arguments on the queen;
and the man who finally went to Lambeth was Bishop Potter of
Oxford – 'whose capacity is not so good,' Hervey said to Walpole,
'nor his temper so bad, as to make you apprehend any great
danger in his being there'.

William Cole, the Cambridge antiquary who knew Sherlock
and the Walpole family, recorded a judgment of Hare which is
scarcely less severe. 'That the bishop was of a sharp and
piercing wit, of great judgment and understanding in worldly
matters, and of no less sagacity and penetration in matters of
learning, and especially of criticism, is sufficiently clear from the
works he has left behind him; but that he was of a sour and
crabbed disposition is equally manifest.'

The point is borne out by a family miniature preserved in

Francis Hare

Memorials of a Quiet Life, a delightful book chiefly about Hare's
great-grandson Augustus and his wife (and brought out in 1872
by their nephew, Augustus J. C. Hare). The miniature shows
the bishop to have had fierce, wide eyes set in a round face
under black eyebrows and a black wig. Augustus was a young
philosophy don from New College, Oxford, who between 1829
and his death in 1834 buried himself in the tiny parish of Alton
Barnes in the Vale of Pewsey to bring the comforts of the
Christian faith to a handful of illiterate rustics. The contrast
between worldliness in one period of the Church of England's
life and re-emergent idealism in another could hardly be more
marked.

Francis Hare applied his linguistic skill narrowly. He deployed
it at home: his son by his first wife, as a boy at the castle, was
made to speak Greek 'as his ordinary language in the family'. (It
did him little good: he led a wild life as a young man, being a
member of the Hell Fire Club at Medmenham, and grieved his
father by insisting on an engagement to his step-aunt, the
bishop's second wife's sister. He married her after his father's
death.) But Hare took care not to unleash his scholarly aptitudes on the New Testament: he was too well aware that to
suggest 'that some passages are *interpolated,* or that some
celebrated texts are not genuine, or should be otherwise read,
or have not been *rightly understood,* or do not prove the point they
are commonly brought for', could ruin a man professionally.
(He himself triumphantly escaped ruin for saying so. The
Church's Parliament, Convocation, disliked the scepticism as
well as the too-overt worldliness of Hare's *Letter on the Difficulties
and Discouragements which attend the Study of the Scriptures in the way
of Private Judgment,* in which that passage appears, and censured
the author; but the very next year he began his swift ascent by
way of the deanery of Worcester.) The nearest he came to
biblical studies was to publish, while he was at Chichester, an
edition of the Psalms in the original Hebrew; but thirty years
later he was found by another scholar to have got his theory of
Hebrew versification wrong. Even his scholarship was quarrel-
some. He compared notes with Bentley, the great Latinist of the

age; but their friendship turned to bile when Hare brought out an edition of Terence, the Roman comic playwright, which used points out of letters from Bentley – who had meant to produce an edition of his own. Bentley retaliated in kind: knowing that Hare was meditating an edition of Phaedrus (a Roman Aesop), he rushed out his own version. Hare delightedly discovered errors committed in haste, and excoriated them in an open letter – in Latin – to the headmaster of Eton. *Odium academicum* was his life blood.

Hare is a figure perfectly of his era. Swift exchanged epithets with him; Pope threw him half a line in the *Dunciad* as the type of a worthy preacher whom the age neglected; Thackeray resurrected him as a scrap of period detail. And he left behind him four crown octavo volumes of contentious sermons and pamphlets.

The sermons show him to have been, in line with most clerics of the time, an authoritarian. The cure for the self-indulgence of the age, he believed, as he perceived it in other people, was regular punishment. ('A succession of punishments coming thick upon one another, if a lewd house be incessantly pursued by the hand of justice, till it is either abandoned or reformed, will break the hearts of the most obstinate offenders, and force them either to leave their houses or their wicked courses.') He was fond of preaching from the verses in Romans 13 which declared that rulers, as a terror to evil, were ordained of God. There had been no case, in his view, even for rising against Charles I, let alone for beheading him. Yet the same deference was due the house of Stuart's successors. The encomia bestowed on Anne were rolled out again for George I ('a prince who, by a wise and just and steady government of another country for many years, has shown in how high a degree he possesses all the virtues requisite to make us a happy people, if it be not our own fault') and George II ('who has no interest separate from that of his people, no views but to promote their welfare, no glory but in their prosperity').

Hare carried the same authoritarianism into the affairs of the Church. It must be the mistress of its own doctrines. 'To the question "Who shall interpret?" I answer, not a single pastor by his mere authority, but in every Church the governors of it, assisted by the best lights they can get, and with a particular regard to the sense of the primitive Church where it can be had.' Nonconformists, certainly, had nothing to say in the matter: their deviant private judgment was often merely uninformed; many of them had not even read the Prayer Book. More importantly, the State had no competence either. That was among Hare's points when he took part in one of the famous Church rows of the century: the Bangorian controversy.

It was about the old issue, the quarrel which the Restoration settlement had done so little to end: how far the Church's forms of belief and worship were immutable. Under George I, Tory high-churchmen in Hare's mould began to feel themselves beleaguered. The activists on their side were the non-jurors – unyielding divine-rightists who, having taken an oath of allegiance to James II, would neither say the same words for William III nor resign. They had lost their jobs, but they formed a separate sect within Anglicanism which survived, dwindling, throughout the eighteenth century. In 1716 they published a claim that all who were not with them were outside the true Church. It came from the posthumous papers of George Hickes, a royalist and Anglo-Saxon grammarian, who had followed the tough old Edward Layfield as vicar of All Hallows. Hickes had been promoted from there to the deanery of Worcester, deprived of it for non-juring, and finally consecrated by like-minded bishops to the fictitiously revived see of Thetford.

Hickes's challenge from beyond the grave was answered by Benjamin Hoadly, a newly appointed bishop of Bangor; and the prolonged resulting row took the name of his see, even though in six years as bishop he never went near it. His peculiarity was that a crippling illness as a young man obliged him to preach kneeling. It gave him an appearance of sanctity he did not altogether deserve: he was in fact an ecclesiastical careerist in Hare's own class. While he was bishop of Bangor he held on to two London benefices at once, and was then swiftly translated through two further bishoprics until he came to rest in the hugely lucrative see of Winchester. Part of his success came from

cultivating a woman favourite (Mrs Clayton) of the princess
who became Queen Caroline; but he owed most of it to his
usefulness as a controversialist on the Whig side.

His main attack was against any notion that Church leaders
had absolute authority, either in politics or doctrine. The State
had the right to preserve itself against 'persons in ecclesiastical
offices' whose actions threatened it, he said; and a man's title to
God's favour could not depend 'upon his actual being or
continuing in any particular method, but upon his real sincerity
in the conduct of his conscience and of his own actions under it'.
Most Church of England clergymen were outraged. Convocation
began a systematic condemnation of Hoadly. The Whig
Government closed it down; it did not meet again till the 1850s.
A storm of paper controversy was let loose. Two hundred tracts
and pamphlets were published, covering every conceivable
point at issue between high church and low. One of the most
strident pamphleteers was Hare.

As might have been expected, he did not take the high ground.
His attack was conducted in sarcasms about Hoadly's not going
to Bangor (Hare apologizes for publishing the sermon 'at a time
when I had good reason to believe his Lordship's thoughts were
wholly taken up with business of another nature: I mean the
primary visitation of his diocese, whither I concluded he was
gone or going soon; though I find since I was mistaken'); in
thrusts which savaged the chiefly offending publication under
the guise of defending it ('I have often wondered that neither
his Lordship, nor any of his friends, have ever once pleaded
what, in my opinion, is the very best defence that can be made
for it: the great haste and hurry in which it was composed; of
which there are in every part the most visible marks; which
plainly show it not to be the result of his Lordship's maturer
judgment, but a heap of loose, general thoughts, huddled up in a
tumultuary manner, and thrown together for want of time,
without art or order'); and in endless pedantries about Hoadly's
knowledge of Greek.

Hare perceived that Hoadly was in the direct line of descent
from those seventeenth-century forerunners of the age of reason,
Thomas Hobbes and John Locke – 'known enemies to creeds,

and the faith taught in them; which they would reduce into one article, as the most effectual way to sink all revealed religion into what they call natural, and bring down Christianity to mere deism, which shall be just what they please to make it'.

(Deism is the religion of the individual reason: you believe in God because he seems the likeliest explanation of butterflies and sunsets. The problem is that you cannot deduce the whole of Christian teaching in the same way. Locke had actually written a treatise called *The Reasonableness of Christianity as delivered in the Scriptures;* and the 'one article' which he was prepared to accept was that Jesus was the Messiah. But that told the believer nothing about Jesus's identity with God. The questioning of Jesus's divinity is a good deal older even than Locke and the Trinity-doubters whom he encouraged: the Council of Nicaea, in the year 325, was summoned mainly to lay a comparable heresy as propounded by Arius of Alexandria. Hare thought the mere antiquity of Nicaea sufficient answer: 'It is next to giving up Christianity as a cheat and imposture to think God would suffer his Church to err so soon, in so fundamental a point, as they did if the Nicene Council erred in their decisions.')

It was this fierce way with Hoadly, the upholder of Crown rights in the Church, that cost Hare his chaplaincy to George I. But he recovered soon enough when there was a change of monarch. His connection with the new queen was more direct than Hoadly's; and he had not been Walpole's tutor at King's for nothing.

Besides his mention in Swift and Pope and Thackeray, and his four volumes of testy sermons and pamphlets, Hare left behind him one other thing: a small brick mausoleum attached to the south side of the chancel in Chalfont St Giles parish church, covering the vault prepared for his own remains and his family's. It failed of its full effect. When he died, in April 1740, his fellow bishops would not carry him to it as pall-bearers. They were too like him: they refused to leave London in cold weather. Even more sadly, the mausoleum was outlived by the Blandford marble. Hare's great-great-grandson, Augustus J. C. Hare, thought the structure hideous; and it was pulled down in 1861. The demolition disclosed a thirteenth-century lancet window which Hare had blocked up. The then rector filled it with garish stained glass, containing an unidentified memorial mitre; and there is a family tablet below, and the purloined altar-rail hard by. Nothing beside remains. In 1955 the Vache itself, totally altered once again, became a staff college for the National Coal Board.

By the time Hare left Barnes in 1727 for the bishopric of St Asaph, he was also dean of St Paul's. As such he could appoint his own successor in the new rectory. His choice fell on a young man named Robert Kilborn. Kilborn's links with Hare were that he too was by origin an Essex man (his father had been vicar of Saffron Walden), a colleger at Eton, and a don at Cambridge. (His college was Magdalene.)

Kilborn preached in Lambeth chapel at Hare's consecration; and his sermon caught Hare's preoccupations exactly. 'Obedience, esteem and liberality towards the ministers of the Gospel', Kilborn declared, 'are by the apostles frequently enjoined as necessary duties to all Christians'; and it was clear from the rest of the address that, for Kilborn as much as for Hare, the greatest of these was liberality. It had to be secured for the moment by voluntary contributions, but only 'till the governing powers of any society become Christian, who might then, as public persons, do what others had done as private ones, and by the laws of that society settle such a provision, to be raised in such a manner, as they thought most for the honour of God and the real service of the religion they professed themselves members of'. In other words, whatever objection there might be to State control of religion, there was none to State financing of it. Kilborn was in no doubt that it was because endowment gave clerics the leisure to be learned that 'Error has nowhere been more successfully combated, or Christianity more purely taught, or the duties of morality more clearly stated, than by the English clergy'.

Another of Kilborn's few surviving sermons will have been equally gratifying to a twice-married bishop, because it took issue with the notion that the clergy ought to be celibate. 'So irksome a restraint as this', said Kilborn, 'must rob a man of that equanimity which alone leaves him capable either of his own or others' improvement.'

He spoke with feeling. He was only a year married himself, to a girl from across the river at Brentford. Hare had supplied a special licence for the wedding in Barnes church. He looked after Kilborn in more material ways. He made him his chaplain; and he helped him become a prebendary of St Paul's and rector of St Mary Aldermanbury, built not long before by Wren. (Both incumbent and architect would be surprised to see it now – re-erected in the corn plains of Missouri, through the link forged between Winston Churchill and President Harry Truman at the end of the Second World War.)

Kilborn amassed those dignities while he was still at Barnes and barely twenty-nine. All he lacked was Hare's staying-power. He died, after only two years of married equanimity, at thirty.

Samuel Baker, who came to Barnes in 1730 (he had been at Pembroke, Oxford, and was at some stage rector of St Michael's, Cornhill), took Hare the man of business as his pattern. The parish of Barnes was growing rich from the sale of sand and turf carried down river into central London for work at Somerset House or the Temple. Legacies made it richer. Baker – conversant with the City as a member of the St Paul's chapter – was entrusted with some of the money for investment. He laid it out in his own name, and kept the profits. After his death in 1749, several interviews were necessary between the churchwardens and his executor before the money was transferred back to the parish.

3 'I owe my all to your Grace' (1728-1782)

NO ONE HAD MORE TO DO WITH SETTING THE TONE OF the eighteenth-century Church than the duke of Newcastle. He was ignorant, timid, alarmed by anything which hinted at Christian commitment, and of poor judgment: his only skill in politics was as a fixer of votes and elections, and his sole test of merit in bishops was whether they supported the Whigs in the Lords. In return for an income all his adult life of £25,000 a year, his one real service to humanity was to keep nearly all the letters ever written to him. They are a revealing archive. They fill 332 huge red-leather volumes in the British Library; and a high proportion of them are requests for posts in the Church. For Newcastle was put in charge by Walpole, in 1736, of the Government's ecclesiastical patronage; and he kept the job for nearly thirty years.

The great exemplar of the type of churchmanship which Newcastle fostered was a figure who has so far been confined within the decent obscurity of the Newcastle papers: John Hume. He followed Samuel Baker at Barnes. He was a man of no special parts; but he served the duke slavishly, and he became a prince of the Church as a result – on certain terms.

He was the son of a Tiverton cleric; and at Corpus Christi, Oxford, he showed himself a competent scholar. Somehow, early in life, he had achieved an introduction to the duke; and in 1728, when he was twenty-five, he was taken on as travelling tutor in France to Newcastle's elder nephew and heir, a pleasant but sickly child named Lord Clinton. The tutor's totally subordinate relation to both pupil and employer, and his understanding of the family preoccupation with health, shine out from the first. His letters from Aix-en-Provence are of the form: 'May it please your Grace: yesterday I was honoured with your Grace's condescending letter . . . I think I have told your Grace that his Lordship has shook off the little cold which I mentioned . . .'

Hume had plenty to do. In a wavering copperplate the child wrote to his uncle: 'I ride, dance, fence and play, learn Italian, French, Latin and Greek, and I hope in a short time to be able to write you a letter in which of the four languages you please. At present I am in plain English. Your dutiful nephew, George Clinton.' Besides sharing or supervising all this, Hume devised treatments and diets ('I've been obliged to intermit his asses' milk'). The boy's mother, Lady Lincoln, found that Hume had done 'mighty well'. When the pupil nevertheless died, the tutor did not suffer: George was replaced by his younger brother Harry. The new Lord Clinton, too, was sickly: he had a wasted arm, to which 'the muds of Barboutan' were repeatedly applied without much success. By the summer of 1732, at Vigan, Hume was coaching Harry for Eton by dragging him through Virgil, Ovid, Caesar and the Greek New Testament. His Lordship's only faults, Hume reported to the duke, were that he loved finery, and 'I can't say neither that he has a love for his book, though when he is at it he behaves as well as can be expected from one that studies alone.' When the child (by now entitled the earl of Lincoln) went to Eton the next summer, Hume went with him.

Having now served five years in this wholly non-pastoral employment, Hume was held to be in line for a pastoral post; but he applied Newcastle-style standards from the first. The duke asked him if he was interested in the nearby town of Reading. There was not much pretence at pastoral concern. 'In regard to the living of Reading', Hume replied, ''tis not even reckoned above eight score pound a year, and a vast deal of duty to be done for it, so that I should choose not to give your Grace the trouble of asking for it.'

But four years on, when Lord Lincoln went up to Cambridge with his tutor still in tow, fidelity had its first reward. Hume was entrusted with the cure of souls at Toppesfield, in Essex –

though there was no expectation that he would spend much
time there. He had his work cut out with his pupil, who was
drawn by the diversions of his rank. Hume said what could be
said in the young man's defence: 'He has hunted but three
times since he has been here, and though being in company
obliges him to drink more than he has been used to, yet to do
him justice he drinks as little as his situation will permit him.'
The young earl was at Clare, the only college where gates were
shut at eleven in the evening, a restriction which urged Lincoln
to answer the banter of his associates by fitting in as much
dissipation as he could before that hour. But with all this, Hume
was prepared to ask the duke for leave of absence from his
Lordship's side when matters of abiding importance were at
issue. 'As the harvest is now beginning', Hume wrote in July
1738, 'and some of my parishioners disposed to give me trouble
in obliging me to take my tithes in kind, my presence at
Toppesfield would be very necessary, if my attendance on Lord
Lincoln for a little while could be dispensed with.'

By the end of the year Hume was beginning to wonder
whether advancement in the Church was worth the trouble. He
writes to the duke from Cambridge: 'I came here from Toppesfield last Friday, where I have had a great deal of trouble with
the farmers, who will oblige me either to lower the value of my
living very considerably or to take my tithes in kind and go to
law with them. I cannot be sufficiently grateful', he hastens to
add, turning to the duke's offer of an additional parish in
Cambridgeshire, 'but I really find that *one living* is as much as I
can manage consistently with a tolerable share of ease in life,
which makes me wish that your promise of Castle Camps could
be exchanged for something else, though of less value.' Hume
will have been thinking of a cathedral prebend, which paid a
small salary without making any demands about residence.

Lord Lincoln was an increasingly dispiriting charge to stay
with. Hume's tone began to take on a certain edge: 'His
Lordship is in good health and continues to follow his studies
and give me a good deal of his company of evenings, which,
then at least, I am sure he spends soberly.' But that summer,
1739, Lincoln went abroad with a different tutor; and Hume

had the most important promotion of his life. He was transferred
to the service of Newcastle's hypochondriac wife – 'the dear
Dutchess', as she regularly appears in the duke's letters. Hume
remained the intermediary in the constant disputes between
uncle and nephew, but he did as little as he could. A quarter of
a century later the two noble kinsmen were still quarrelling
over the toys of their class: Lincoln was breaking with him, the
duke reported, 'because I propose to take the lieutenancy of
Nottinghamshire myself, and not give it to him'. Hume was a
cautious go-between. 'Nobody knows better what to say', the
duke reproached him, 'if you had courage to bring it out.'
Hume also knew, though, the irresistible excuse: 'I have writ,
as your Grace advised me, to Lord Lincoln, but his answer . . .
has shocked me too much to say anything on the subject. I am
not in a state of health to bear it.'

For the greater part of the 1740s Hume was the duchess's
travelling companion and amanuensis. They went to Bath, where
he enumerated for the duke the number of glasses of the waters
she downed. They went to Buxton, where 'the consultation of
physicians ended in a few grains of myrrh added to her bolus'.
(A bolus was a pill of a size ordinarily administered to horses.)
They travelled to France and Germany. And for the two
following decades the staple of correspondence between the
duke and his liegeman was the dear duchess's health. She
suffered at various times from lumbago, gout in one finger,
lowness of spirits, phlegm on the stomach, trembling of the
hands, hysteria, disorder in the nerves and stomach, cholicky
pain in the bowels, bile and gravel. She clung to these afflictions:
on one occasion Hume reported: 'She has gained much more
use of her hand than she herself is willing to confess, but to all
us it is very visible.'

The topic interested the duke as much as her. There is a
reference in Thomson's *Seasons* to Claremont, near Esher, the
country seat of the Pelhams (Newcastle's family name). He and
his dependants could repair

To Claremont's terraced height, and Esher's groves,
Where, in the sweetest solitude embraced,

> By the soft windings of the silent Mole
> From courts and senates Pelham finds repose.

– But not from the duchess's temperature-charts. Nor did he
want to. They were his abiding interest; and he made sure that
Hume shared it. When the duke and duchess were at Claremont, and Hume was away on such parsonical business as he
could be spared for, the duke pursued him with her medical
records. 'You know how sincerely I interest myself', Hume felt
obliged to write, 'in my Lady duchess's health and happiness,
and therefore how sincerely I am obliged by your frequent
accounts sent me.'

Cunningly, Hume returned the compliment, and when
absence prevented him from writing about the duchess's health
he wrote, knowing his market, about his own: 'I take it for
granted', he once wrote to her, 'that your goodness interests
itself in my health.' He too suffered from lumbago; he also
reported a bad back (treated with 'a warm sticking-plaster'), an
ugly swimming in the head, recurrent bowel trouble, and colds
and sore throats caught preaching.

Writing letters about their complaints was about as thera-
peutic a recourse as mid-eighteenth-century patients had. There
seem to have been extraordinarily few things which Hume or
the duchess could do. They were bled; they took tincture of
rhubarb and salts of wormwood; their remedy of last resort was
the waters. On one occasion when the duke had some unspecified and persistent illness, Hume wrote with all the
solemnity at his command: 'If this disorder should continue,
though for a few days longer only, I must join with the duchess
of Newcastle in insisting that you should set out immediately,
with the least delay, for Bath.'

Thus tactfully subserving the family's ruling passion, Hume
now at last began to harvest his reward. In 1742, when he had in
effect worn the Newcastle livery for fourteen years, the duke had
him made a prebendary of Westminster. A year later he
collected an Oxford doctorate in divinity for no traceable
contribution to learning. In 1747 he preached to the House of
Commons in the additional dignity of chaplain to George II.

He was swiftly transferred from Westminster to St Paul's, where the opportunities were greater. In 1749 he was given, in addition, the St Paul's living of Barnes: he increased the value of it by agreeing with the parish council that he would be exempt from parish rates on his rectory if he buried the poor of the parish (who will not then have been numerous). Soon afterwards he became a residentiary canon, a post worth £800 a year, retaining Barnes; and in 1756 Newcastle had him made bishop of Bristol. Bristol was an ill-paid bishopric, being worth only £450 a year, but by holding on to the canonry and Barnes Hume was able to piece together a livelihood. Two years later the duke translated him to Oxford. The bishopric of Oxford was worth only £50 a year more than Bristol, but Hume took it on from a man who had held it with the deanery of St Paul's (which paid £1800); and passing into both dignities, he was pulling down £2300 a year – a sum which encouraged him to surrender Barnes to an incumbent who would actually live there.

Hume himself now divided his time between his palace in the muddy Oxfordshire countryside at Cuddesdon, where he was dependent for news of the duchess's nerves on letters from the duke dropped off the Birmingham fly at the White Hart at Wheatley, and his deanery in London, where he spent the two or three separate months of his obligatory residence. He perfectly understood that it was the duke of Newcastle rather than the Holy Spirit who had arranged this remarkable eminence. He wrote from Cuddesdon in August 1759: 'My Lord, as your Grace, on taking my leave at Claremont, seemed to hint that a letter from hence would not be unacceptable, I take this first opportunity after going through my diocese to express my gratitude to you for placing me in it. So many favours conferred on me from the beginning of life to this day require more from me in return than I can ever hope to repay. But my Lord, I have a just consciousness of them . . .'

To crown his satisfaction, he was able to add: 'Lady Mary sends her respects.' His first wife, who had the manifestly un-genteel maiden name of Frip, had died during his brief Bristol period. But in the dignity of a bishop he had been able to

Barnes church and rectory from the south, c. 1750

woo and win Lady Mary Hay, a widow richly left, youngest
daughter of the earl of Kinnoull. The earldom was Irish; but
that was still enough to earn her the precious prefix. She bore
the bishop four children. The second, the only boy, became
the duke's godson and in due time an ecclesiastical place-
man on his own account; the three girls all died before their
parents.

Hume was not idle as bishop and dean. Although he deferred
an Oxford ordination for a week because of his lumbago, and
complained of preaching himself hoarse in St Paul's, he did
discharge these formal duties. But unless they pinned him down,
he was the duke's man. Summoned to Claremont, he saw no
choice but to go; and again and again he was to be found
scratching away late at night, in a light which made his eyes
ache, to answer the duke's lightest word by return of post.

Newcastle was a copybook demonstration of the truth that
wealth and power are no guarantees of happiness. He bristled
with self-pity and self-doubt. He was obsessed with lack of
regard shown to him, by successive kings whom he professed to
serve, by relatives for whom he had done favours, even by
bishops whom he had appointed and who now refused to make
lesser appointments according to his wishes. This sense of
desertion was heightened by the frequency with which even the
dear duchess left him for her bedroom. 'My dearest Lord,' he
wrote from Claremont to Cuddesdon one August during one of
her attacks of lumbago, 'if she does not mend in a short time I
shall beg that you would come up to us for a few days and
comfort me; for I am now so reduced that I have not only one
sincere friend but yourself.' And in the end Hume put off his
Michaelmas ordination and went.

Beyond that, the duke demanded certain spiritual reassur-
ances. In particular, quintessentially Anglican figure as he was,
he wanted to be certified that you could be a Christian without
any marked degree of commitment – without any very earnest
striving after good conduct, or any regular practice of the faith,
or any serious attempt to come to grips with its doctrines; and
all this, of course, the bishop was happy to confirm. Good
intentions were quite enough: 'Let me entreat you, my dear

Lord, to compose your mind and be assured that the wish to do right is right.' The duke was especially troubled about taking communion: he had a sense that it should be done in a 'worthy' frame of mind, but was not disposed when it came to the point to make the needed mental effort, even for the few times each year which were all that custom then enjoined.

The bishop vapidly abetted this sloth. 'If you determine on reflection, and from humility, to omit it, you have no reason to be uneasy; but if on the same motives you determine to do it, you have reason to be happy.' Even the term 'communion' was shyly avoided between them, as savouring too much of zeal: flat circumlocutions were substituted. 'I am under some doubt about doing this Whit Sunday', wrote the duke, 'what I had before determined upon.' His mind was taken up, he explained, with a change of government, his problems with a politician he deplored, William Pitt – 'the same quarter that all difficulties arise' – and the question of his ministerial status (though not of course on his own account: it was the dear duchess, he explained, who was 'mighty desirous that I should have the Privy Seal'). The bishop replied in the same coy vein. 'All things considered, as Michaelmas is not *very* distant, perhaps it may be as well to defer this affair till then.' When Michaelmas came, of course, the duke was still preoccupied with the inconsiderateness of Pitt and his own relatives; and 'This makes me so uneasy, and employs my thoughts so much, that if you have no objection to it I have thoughts (especially as you can't be here) to defer doing what I otherwise ought to do Christmas.' The bishop had indeed no objection.

The duke had an inkling that the faith was a serious matter, and yet shrank from taking it seriously. He wanted instruction, but in course of conversation; or if through the written word, then 'without going too deep'. He had that phrase from the archbishop of York, and Hume approved it too. 'I have spent more time in thinking than in reading,' he claimed to the duke, 'and in considering things themselves than in following other men's thoughts of them. I am not therefore so capable to point out a proper course of reading to your Grace, because I have not read all that perhaps I ought to have read myself . . . But my

Lord, I really think you read as much as is necessary for you. Religion does not consist in *reading*.'

The bishop's sermons bear out that estimate of himself all too well. Four survive. They were perfunctorily published, by the public bodies over which they were preached; and perfunctorily written, according to an unvarying formula by which he first set himself two questions and then answered them. They give off in consequence a strong sense of a man merely spinning sentences till his time is up. They are not in any real sense Christian: they contain no doctrine; they are largely made up of sententious and satisfied observations on human life as it is. Power is given to men of rank, he told the noble governors of the London Hospital, 'and we have no reason to doubt of his wisdom who dispenses it'. The blessing of God is on George III's arms, he told the Society for the Propagation of the Gospel in Foreign Parts: the evidence he offered was that 'they have made the most distant countries accessible to our missionaries'. He saw no conflict between that defence of empire and his assertion a few years earlier (castigating Cromwell in the annual Westminster Abbey sermon on the martyrdom of Charles I) that every man's rights and liberty were 'marked out to him in the reasons and nature of things', and if we tried to extend our own, 'the attempt is wickedness, the result anarchy and confusion'.

But the duke required other services from his protégé besides spiritual counsel; and these demands became more pressing after his final favour to Hume, which was to have him translated in 1766 from Oxford and St Paul's to a post which (at £3000 a year) outpaid the pair of them: the bishopric of Salisbury.

The appointment was made easy because George III himself suggested it to Newcastle – though the duke discovered that in making it he lost the loyalty of relatives (who had wanted the job for dependants of their own) and of other bishops he had created (who no longer had that further preferment to look to). Patronage was not all pleasure. For Hume and Lady Mary, at any rate, joy was at first unconfined. An excited note from Hume to the duke about a mysterious summons to Lambeth was followed by a letter which ran: 'I must now, the first moment I have, express the deep and lasting sense I have of my great obligations to you . . . As long as I live I shall feel myself yours and my Lady duchess's most obliged, grateful, devoted, and – if I might have leave to say it – affectionate humble servant, J. Oxford.' His next letter acknowledged, truly enough: 'I owe my all to your Grace.'

By the time Hume could sign himself 'J. Sarum', and was able to look into essentials, his rapture was modified. He had to pay more than £500 for furniture already in the palace. Worse, 'I am sorry to find one thing by looking into the accounts of the bishopric, that my predecessor in the space of four years has had the luck of receiving the common profits of at least seven, and of filling up all the best preferment in the patronage.' The house was large, he allowed, and the garden very large – nearly twenty-five acres; but it was 'low, level and damp'.

The duke dismissed the domestic details with the charmless humour of the very rich: 'As to your little *fiddle-faddles* of furnishing and unfurnishing palaces, etcetera, you must forgive me if I don't much enter into them.' He had weightier expectations of this new potentate of his own creation.

In part he needed the bishop simply as lobby-fodder in the Lords. Sometimes Hume could discharge his obligation by giving a proxy vote to a brother bishop who could be relied on to vote the Newcastle interest. But proxies were not allowed in committee. In 1767 the duke was anxious about the committee progress of a Bill restricting the legislative freedom of the American colonies. Through the duchess, he asked expressly for Hume's attendance; and he added in a separate letter: 'I own I should be extremely mortified, and I think exposed, if you did not comply with my request.' Hume had unspecified troubles of his own; he nevertheless saw nothing for it but to write back the same day from his house off Regent Street: 'Ill able as I am to support myself under my present unhappiness, with an infirm body and broken spirits, yet if your Grace and my Lady duchess command me, I certainly will attend . . . I hoped indeed that . . . I might have been excused . . . but your Grace cannot excuse me, and I submit.'

In part the bishop was now useful as a source of patronage on his own account. As a lesser bishop he had run errands on the

duke's behalf to potentates like the bishop of London and the
archbishop of Canterbury. At Oxford, although the duke had
sometimes asked his help in securing a living or a fellowship,
Hume's influence was so slight that he had been able to plead
incapacity. But at Salisbury, where he had prebends and
livings in his direct gift, he found himself regularly beset, both
by the duke and the duke's dependants. A sad example was the
Talbot affair.

Talbot was a young fellow of Clare and a chaplain of the
duke's. Within a month of Hume's appointment to Salisbury,
the duke commended Talbot to him. 'It will be a pleasure to me
to serve Mr Talbot', Hume replied: 'he is your Grace's friend
and a man of worth and character'; and he unwisely promised
that Talbot should have the first 'good thing' that came up.
Less than a year later, the duke found it necessary to issue a
reminder: 'I am sure I need not put your Lordship in mind of
my very deserving chaplain Mr Talbot.' Given this insistence,
it was unwise of Hume to hope that – when the first paying post
fell vacant at Salisbury three months later – he could nevertheless
bestow it on a nephew of his own (a fellow of Merton named
James Hume Spry); and doubly unwise to take the precaution
of telling the duke his intention. 'There is a small prebend in my
church', he wrote deprecatingly, 'now vacant, the *clear* annual
value of which is about £16 per annum, *not worth offering to
Mr Talbot*, which I therefore intend giving to my nephew with
your Grace's leave.'

The duke at once brought heavy persuasion to bear. Not
merely were the duchess's bowels giving trouble, and her hands,
and the duke's own ungrateful nephews; but his secretary (a
cleric named Hurdis, who deserves at least part of the credit for
the voluminousness of the Newcastle archive) was ill, and the
only replacement whom the duke had been able to summon was
Talbot. 'For this reason of convenience to myself, as well as in
consequence of my promise to him, I must beg your Lordship
would give him the small vacant prebend; it will be an earnest
of better preferment when it falls' – in other words, of a
residentiary canonry later. Hume was asked to do nothing about
the prebend till the duke knew Talbot's wishes.

John Hume

Hume, just off to count the duchess's imbibings at Bath, replied glumly: 'In obedience to your Grace's commands I have suspended the disposal of the prebend, though I had promised it to my nephew, and the instruments were actually drawn.'

The duke's acknowledgment is classic evidence for the frankly feudal structure of the eighteenth-century Church. He had now persuaded himself that the prebend was not the small thing Hume had maintained, but rightly considered was the first instalment on an inseparable larger offering. 'I am much obliged to your Lordship', he wrote, 'for postponing the disposition of the small prebend; but give me leave to say, you are not quite explicit upon that head. The promise you was so good as to make me was of the first good thing that should fall for Mr Talbot. By all I can find, a prebend, and canonry, is the best thing we can hope for; and though the canonry is not *strictly* in your Lordship's gift, yet I shall be satisfied with this prebend, and an assurance from you that Mr Talbot shall have your recommendation to the chapter for the first canonry that shall fall.

'You must not be surprised that I am so pressing. But at a time when my nearest relations have deserted me . . . you must not be surprised that I should press those of my friends the bishops who have it in their power to reward my deserving friends in the university when I have no other way but through them of doing it.' (Though out of office, Newcastle was chancellor at Cambridge, and enjoyed it; but he needed votes to sustain his position, and therefore the power to do favours to buy them with.)

He went on to upbraid two bishops, Lichfield and Chichester, as traitors to the Newcastle interest; but there were others who had remembered their creator. 'The bishops of Durham and Worcester have done it, *amply*; the archbishop of York and bishop of Lincoln as far as has been in their power; and my good friend the bishop of Norwich, who is a very small patron, has destined one of his best preferments that way if it falls.' And to underline the bishop of Salisbury's vassalage still further, the duke asked for his proxy for a Lords vote.

Hume, after first dutifully reporting the Duchess's score at

Bath, defended himself as best he could. He had been perfectly frank about the prebend's real value, he contended: it was not a good thing, and was not likely to turn into one, since he had not the least reason to think that his recommendation to the chapter for any subsequent canonry would succeed. However, protesting his loyalty, he sent the necessary form for Talbot to fill in. It turned out that Talbot had gone back to Clare. As a final humiliation, Hume had to write to him there to tell him that the prebend was his if he would come and pick it up.

Yet Hume won in the end. The duke died the following year, 1768. In 1770 James Hume Spry became vicar of Potterne, a living in the bishop's diocese and gift. In 1773 he added another such, Brixton Deverill. In 1774, by a move which must have given the bishop intense satisfaction, Spry became a prebendary of the cathedral. This first prebend could not be counted a 'good thing': it was worth only £3 a year. But Newcastle had been right in his suspicion that one thing could lead to another. The following year Spry was shifted to a prebend worth £32 a year; and he kept his two Wiltshire livings besides.

With Newcastle dead, Hume was at peace. He had no further prospect of advancement, but he had no one who could give him orders either. The stick was put away along with the carrot; and for the last fourteen years of his life he could enjoy being a highly-placed prelate. He visited Salisbury from time to time to ordain, and on one occasion to have George III and Queen Charlotte to stay at his palace. But he spent much of his life in London, and died there at the age of seventy-eight. He is buried in the cathedral's south transept, where two memorial tablets tell the story of his immediate family.

In the great hall of the cathedral choir school, which was the palace of the bishops of Salisbury from the eleventh century till 1947, are the portraits of a whole bevy of seventeenth- and eighteenth-century bishops. By far the best picture is the one of Hume: it is attributed to Sir William Beechey, portrait painter to Queen Charlotte. It shows him in a slate-blue frock coat with buttoned cuffs, a sculptured silver wig like a big helmet, and the badge of chancellor of the order of the Garter. A late-nineteenth-century bishop, John Wordsworth, used to point out

Hume's 'keen and acquisitive features'. It is certainly not a holy face; but it is unmarked by self-indulgence, and it is not without humour. It is the face of a man who seems to dare the spectator to expose him.

His influence, like Lady Mary, lived after him. It expressed itself in just the way he would have wished. His son – the duke's godson – became in due time canon treasurer of the cathedral. Two of the canon treasurer's sons slid into episcopal livings not far away; a third, a fellow of King's, became chaplain to a Wiltshire landowner, the marquis of Ailesbury. Service was a family tradition.

4 'Infidelity, popery and enthusiasm' (1729-1768)

THE CLEAR WEAKNESS OF THE SYSTEM BY WHICH HUME had lived, based as it was entirely on connections, was that any link between promotion and merit was accidental. Some able people were promoted; but so were a number of incompetents, and – perhaps more seriously – a certain amount of talent was wasted, to the detriment both of its possessors and of the people they might have served.

While Hume was rector of Barnes, his most distinguished parishioner was Henry Fielding; and during that same time, as tenant of a fine flat-fronted house which still overlooks Barnes pond, Fielding was at work on his last book, *Amelia*. In the course of the novel an elderly parson named Dr Harrison, who clearly speaks for Fielding himself, describes it as 'an infamous scandal on the nation' that there should be men of excellent merit and qualifications who cannot feed their families. A peer, a man with jobs in his gift, asks incredulously how it would be possible to provide for all men of merit. 'Only by not providing for those who have none', says Harrison: 'the men of merit in any capacity are not, I am afraid, so extremely numerous that we need starve any of them, unless we wickedly suffer a set of worthless fellows to eat their bread.'

The sentiment will have been fervently echoed by the man who between 1758 and 1768 followed Hume at Barnes. His name was Ferdinando Warner. He deserved better of the Church of England than Hume did, and fared worse. He was a great deal more interested than Hume in the content, as distinct from the forms or the rewards, of true belief; he did his best to tolerate departures from it; he gave voice to those concerns in

far greater industry as a writer and preacher than Hume ever
showed. He was even a match for Hume as an amateur doctor.
More than that, these qualities were known to the man that
mattered: the duke of Newcastle. Yet the chance alchemy of
patronage never transmuted him. He ended his days in Barnes
rectory.

Warner was born in the same year as Hume – 1703. Like
Hume, he had a number of clerical relatives (one of them a
bishop); and of his five children, at least one became a parson.
By 1729, after he had gone down from Jesus, Cambridge, he was
curate at Borden in Kent. By 1737 he was vicar of Whitchurch
in Hampshire, and so underpaid that he became worried about
his family, and mooted a fund 'for the better maintenance of the
widows and children of the clergy'. By 1748 he was rector of a
St Paul's living in the City, now disappeared, called St Michael,
Queenhithe. In each of these posts he was invited to preach
special sermons – to the naval officers in His Majesty's chapel at
Sheerness, to the Hampshire clergy at the time of their annual
visit from their bishop, to the Lord mayor and aldermen of
London. The Queenhithe post was also ill-paid and carried no
rectory: Warner lived at Lewisham, and made up his income
with what he could earn at a privately-owned chapel in Great
Queen Street, on the eastern edge of Covent Garden.

He was a busy maker or compiler of books. He undertook
them, he repeatedly said in dedications and prefaces, out of a
sense of duty – 'with a view of doing some service to my
country', or as 'a service to religion and letters here at home'.
His alternative explanation was that he was importuned by his
friends. His first book was nothing less than a complete guide to
correct belief and conduct, in five volumes. It was published in
1750. Warner called it *A System of Divinity and Morality*; and he
put it together by the simple expedient of collecting and
arranging 133 sermons preached by most of the great divines of
the Church of England since Tillotson and Stillingfleet. There
were sermons on the creed, and sermons on minding one's own
business. At the end of the fifth volume he included a sermon of
his own, which compared the iniquities of London – and its
likely future fate – to those of Nineveh in the book of Jonah. He

was anxious to dispel any idea that putting the book together had been easy: 'it has required great labour and pains; for great numbers of volumes were to be perused'. The collection might be useful, he thought, 'to all such of the inferior clergy, whose income being small, have scarce a sufficiency to maintain their families, much less to purchase books'; they might even care to preach some of the sermons themselves. And if heads of families would read one of the sermons to their children and servants every Sunday evening, 'we might in time hope to have revived at least the appearance of religion in these kingdoms'.

He followed this enterprise two years later with another volume of other men's sermons, all hitting at popery: he called it *A Rational Defence of the English Reformation and Protestant Religion*. In 1754 he came out with an annotated edition (he called it an 'illustration') of the Book of Common Prayer: it was published in weekly parts, so that families could buy it, and then bound up into a lectern-sized volume which would be 'a very useful book to fix in our parish churches, our hospitals, and houses of charity'. On the title-page of the bound edition, the letters 'M.A.' after Warner's name have been covered with a tiny printed sticker which records a new academic dignity: 'LL.D.', or doctor of laws. The next year he published an answer to a lately dead philosopher-politician, Lord Bolingbroke, who had maintained that the Old Testament was a merely human document – 'delivered to us on the faith of a superstitious people, among whom the custom and art of pious lying prevailed remarkably'; and since Warner cast the book in dialogue form, half the book was lifted from Bolingbroke's own writings and the other half derived from answers to him already published. Warner's next work, also dating from 1755, *A Free and Necessary Enquiry* into whether the Church of England might not be showing too much tolerance towards the doctrine of transubstantiation, was similarly pieced together. ('My next authority is the learned Whitby . . . Let us now hear what the able divine Archbishop Sharp says on this subject . . .') And his memoir of Sir Thomas More, in 1758, was no more than an introduction to a new edition of the earlier translation of *Utopia* by Bishop Gilbert Burnet. Warner's first book of his own, published in 1759, was a *History of England as it relates to Religion and the Church*. It was in two volumes; and the second was dedicated to the duke of Newcastle.

It was an age when writers made what they could of dedications. Warner's *Rational Defence* had been dedicated to the archbishop of Canterbury; his Prayer Book commentary to the Prince of Wales; his *Bolingbroke* to an aristocratic lawyer acquaintance; his *More* to Sir Robert Henley, Lord Keeper of the Great Seal; and the first volume of the church *History* to the king himself, George II. All these men could help Warner in his profession; and Newcastle above all.

The duke knew Warner's name before this. Warner has his place in the long red row of volumes which house the duke's correspondence. Since Warner first came to London he had been a suitor to the duke through intermediaries; and by 1753 he was writing direct, declaring: 'I have no ambition, my Lord; I have no avarice; but a wife and five children, entirely unprovided for, give me desires which I should not otherwise have.' By 1756 the tone was already a hardened suitor's, emboldened by impatience. 'My Lord', Warner wrote, 'I hope you will excuse my acquainting you that the rector of *Munden in Hertfordshire* is now certainly dead. This living is in His Majesty's gift.' The letter ran through Warner's deserts: his attachment to the royal family and the Whigs, his numerous children, 'some little reputation' as a writer, his scheme for a widows' fund. Hope deferred maketh the heart sick, he quoted, and his had been for many years deferred. 'I have but this moment received this intelligence; I have no time to study for expressions; the heart and not the understanding has spoke to you in this letter.'

He did not go to Munden. He was not made chaplain at Lincoln's Inn when that post fell vacant in 1757, though his need was now increased: his income had been halved by the sale, over his head, of the Great Queen Street chapel – where he had been 'ten years preacher to a congregation which four judges and six members of Parliament frequented; and I have all my life supported the present Government, and a Whig administration, with zeal and firmness'. He was not appointed to a prebend at Canterbury or Westminster, his fallback suggestion. He missed a prebend at Canterbury again the next year, when he wrote to the duke: 'In all probability there will be a vacancy within a few days at Canterbury; I had a letter from thence yesterday, that Dr Holcomb, who is above eighty, was extremely ill, and not likely to live a week . . .'

He had no success two months later, when he had been reduced to importuning the duchess's companion for help, and had a new reason for needing it: 'Mrs Spence, my Lord, having informed me that she had been so kind as to remind your Grace of what I was persuaded had slipped out of your mind, and that your Grace had been good enough to say that you would make your acknowledgment to me for my dedication as you always had intended, I thought I might acquaint your Grace without impropriety that your favour would be doubly acceptable to me just at this juncture, as I have the great expense of a dispensation etc. to discharge next week for the living of Barnes, which my Lord Keeper has been so extremely kind to bestow upon me; and as I had not an opportunity of seeing your Grace this morning, I shall wait upon you again on Thursday, and am, my Lord, your Grace's most obedient and most devoted humble servant, Ferdo. Warner.'

Warner had lately become the Lord Keeper's chaplain: the appointment followed the dedication of the More memoir. The post may have been no special pleasure: the Lord Keeper, by now ennobled as Lord Henley, was more generally known as Surly Bob; but he carried enough weight with the dean and chapter of St Paul's to secure for Warner the living of Barnes. (The dispensation which Warner had to pay for was from the notional rule against plurality. Warner was holding on to Queenhithe, though Barnes became his home.) Warner's one piece of good fortune did not come to him from the duke.

There may have been reasons why he found no favour. He was not a wholly attractive figure: he had his share of petulant self-importance. His most remarkable work is an exercise in covert advertisement which would strike even a twentieth-century public-relations man with a sneaking envy. He published, anonymously, an eighteenpenny booklet called *Advice from a Bishop*. It purported to be a collection of nine letters from

an Irish bishop, lately dead, to a young relative on the point of
taking orders; and for a while it passed as such. It was in fact a
sustained puff for Warner's books, and a protest against their
sluggish sales. It began with the *History*.

'I had a great desire,' writes the pseudo-bishop, 'about a year
ago, to encourage a work which I imagined would be extremely
useful to all young clergymen especially, and at the same time
not unedifying nor unentertaining to the old. I mean the church
history of England, which I have so often mentioned to you,
undertaken by Dr Warner . . . who, though a stranger to me,
yet from his public labours in the service of the Church and of
religion was entitled, I thought, to the patronage of men of
letters and in particular of the bishops and clergy.' Advance
subscriptions for the book, though, he goes on, had been so
small as to convict the clergy of ignorance and sloth.

Warner was in that a little hard. Subscriptions – promises of
purchase – may have been difficult to get at first: they were
deferred till the second volume; but by the time that was
published, the list printed in it included the Prince of Wales,
both archbishops, the headmaster of Eton (who bought two
copies), several bishops (one of them Hume, despite his
declared coolness towards reading), Surly Bob and the actor
David Garrick.

Warner quoted at length from his *History*, in a passage about
the shocking way in which livings were currently bought and
sold. In further letters he pressed the claims of his Prayer Book
commentary ('It will be highly necessary that you should study
some of the best illustrations of the Common Prayer,' he wrote,
knowing that his own was the only one in print); of his *System*
('You may safely have recourse to the modern systems of
divinity', where he had a similar monopoly); and of his
Bolingbroke ('For the proof of revelation against the attacks on
unbelievers', he recommended, 'you may confine yourself to
what hath been written by the late Lord Bolingbroke on the one
side, and to his answerers on the other': the Warner book was
unique in bringing both sides within the same set of covers).

In the *Advice* he spoke up for himself as a performer, too,
since nobody else would. He had seen only two English divines

use any 'action', or gestures, in the pulpit, he wrote: they were the only real preachers he had come across; and one of them 'took as much pains, he told me, in writing and speaking his sermon in his study before he preached it as most others do in the composition; and his success was answerable'. If Warner had had a name to drop at that point, he would have dropped it. This action man must have been himself; and the other was probably his son John.

Warner went on to say that the voice must be appropriately modulated in the prayers, and not dropped at the end of the sentence. This implication that plain technical incompetence was at least as rife among the clergy then as it is now was buttressed with evidence. There was little theological training at Oxford or Cambridge, Warner said: 'a candidate for orders comes to the bishop as ignorant of the religion he is to teach, and as unable to prove the truth of it, as the meanest mechanic he is to instruct.' Warner's advice to young men (for which there was precedent in men he admired like Burnet) was that they should start by preaching other men's sermons. That was partly why he had reissued so many himself.

Yet if Warner was as meritorious, both in writing and preaching, as he clearly believed himself to be, why had he not had more success in his profession? He wrote the *Advice* partly to provide himself with an answer to that uncomfortable question. The fact was, he argued, that preferment was most easily had by 'mean and dirty ways'. Young men entered the ministry 'only with a view to get a maintenance without any trouble'. Livings were bought and sold like estates. Economic pressure might sometimes oblige a man to hold more than one living, true, and therefore be non-resident in one of them; but it became 'a matter of ill-desert and scandal', Warner protested, 'for the clergy to live in the capital of the kingdom about half the year it may be, doing nothing and having nothing to do but to indulge themselves in amusements and idle curiosity, or to frequent the levées of the great for the sake of mere preferment. This is a non-residence which is so far from being necessary in the Church that it is unjust and scandalous.'

Yet he had himself been seen at Newcastle's levées – his

morning audiences; and even though Warner told himself that promotion won on those terms was not worth having, he missed it painfully. 'You know with what integrity', he wrote in the last letter of the book, 'and with what good intentions, I have always pursued the truth in my enquiries; and that I desired to bear witness to it in such a manner as to give no just offence to the "powers that be"; and yet you likewise know' – and here the poor man broke off, pretending, with the editorial phrase '*desunt nonnulla*', that something was missing from the manuscript as it had gone to the printers; when in fact the missing sentiment was one he could not write without discarding both his sense of shame and his momentary disguise, for it would have been that Ferdinando Warner had never become a dignitary of the Church.

He went on to maintain that ecclesiastics who 'scraped up many thousands out of the revenues of the Church of Christ' (and he instanced a 'B——— H———' who may be taken to be Bishop Hoadly) called its whole teaching into question when they so flouted its recommendation to unworldliness. 'But be this to themselves', he concluded, still seeking to persuade himself that he had freed his own soul from any such preoccupations: '*liberavi animam meam.*'

In July of the year in which the book was published, 1759, he was once more beginning a letter to the duke from Barnes: 'My Lord, as I see this morning by the papers that there is a vacancy made in the church of Canterbury by the death of Dr Young . . .' To the earl of Hardwicke, the following May: 'Having been informed last night of a vacancy at Windsor by the death of Mr Blacon . . .' And to the duke again four months after that: 'My Lord, I saw just now in the papers that Mr Meadowcourt, a prebendary of Worcester, is dead . . .' Freedom in the soul was a quality which tended to fade.

Warner's style as a religious writer combined this streak of self-importance with the implication, which he learned from the divines whose sermons he anthologized, that the Christian faith was a perfectly sensible and comprehensible thing if it was properly explained, as the evangelists had not always explained it. His Prayer Book commentary accompanies the lesson set down for each day with a paraphrase. The first verse of the gospel for Christmas day ('In the beginning was the Word, and the Word was with God, and the Word was God') reads in the Warner version: 'In order to give an account of the manner of God's manifesting himself by the gospel, for the redemption and salvation of mankind, it will be proper to begin with a description of the person by whom this great salvation was effected. With God the Father therefore there existed, before all ages, that divine person whose name is called *the Word of God*; and this Word was not only present with the Father, the fountain of the deity, throughout all those infinite ages, but was himself likewise very God.' St John and his translators in the Authorized Version score seventeen words, nearly all short, against Warner's eighty-nine. His printer squeezes the paraphrase in, downpage, by using very small type.

Yet on the evidence of what he wrote Warner was neither more nor less learned, neither more nor less capable a minister, than many men who in the lottery of promotion became canons and deans and bishops. He typified the instructed Anglican of his time. In the eighteenth century, the most active religious ideas were two. One was Arian. From the beginning of the century there were professing Christians who questioned the doctrine of the Trinity: they doubted whether Christ was divine (though they believed in God, which is why they could be called deists). The other was Evangelical: it laid a new emphasis on personal commitment and fervour, and its principal eighteenth-century exponents were the Methodists. Warner, a mainstream Anglican, spent his life resisting both – as well as Roman Catholicism, the old enemy. Deists were simply infidels, in his view, and Methodists displayed an un-Anglican enthusiasm which could decline – through a stress on right belief above right conduct – into a lack of moral principle. At the beginning of his writing life (in the preface to his 1750 *System*) Warner declared that 'deism, popery and immorality reign triumphant in our nation'. Near the end (varying the names of the two new targets for the preface to a 1767 edition) he gave it as the book's aim 'to stem the torrent of infidelity, popery and enthusiasm which are deluging our country'.

Ostensibly, like all the divines whose sermons he borrowed in the *System*, he took reason as his guiding star. The book was an enquiry 'whether there be in reason and argument, and in the nature of things, any true and just grounds to believe the general and most common principles of natural and revealed religion, or not'. The sermons in it had titles like 'The usefulness and reasonableness of divine faith' (that was Tillotson), or 'The incarnation of Christ agreeable to natural reason' and 'The reasonableness of the terms of salvation' (both Stillingfleet). But reason could go too far. A sermon of Richard Bentley's, also included, caught Warner's attitude to the deists exactly: we value reason as much as they do, Bentley said, but it was by the benefit of reason 'that when we departed from the errors of popery we knew where to stop'.

Warner was in fact bored by the too free play of reason, by what he called 'learned and useless controversies'. One of his earliest published sermons was preached at Andover, in 1737, before an assemblage of the local clergy gathered for 'the annual visitation of the Lord bishop of Winchester', their diocesan. The bishop at the time was none other than Hoadly, the man who believed that there was no reliable way of attaining to correct belief, and all that mattered was the actions dictated by a sincere conscience. Taking this cue, Warner poured scorn on 'abstruse and unintelligible questions or opinions which terminate in speculation only'. Instead of subtle and mysterious systems, 'our blessed Saviour has only recommended, in the most elegant simplicity, the laws of truth and righteousness' (as if there were no difficulty about keeping those laws, and no diversity of indications in the Bible about what happens to us when we break them).

Released from Hoadly's supervision, Warner showed a little more interest in theology; but he still regarded theological speculation as essentially impertinent. Human beings should mind their own business. ('Presume not God to scan', as Pope had ruled a little earlier.) In his *History* he wrote, when he came to the outbreak of the Trinitarian controversy at the start of the century: 'Indeed the minds of men were so much inflamed, and their animosities so much excited by this controversy, that it would have been well for the world and for Christianity if they would have taken things as they found them; and being convinced that God is able to explain himself to the world, as far as he thinks it convenient, so where he hath not used this perspicuity, that they would check their curiosity and content themselves without it. The great doctrine of the Trinity, so universally allowed to be the greatest mystery in our religion, could never surely be intended for debate and controversy; and being a subject incomprehensible, it must necessarily be a subject very unmeet for disputation among frail and short-sighted men. It is one of the deep things of God among a thousand others which he hath been pleased to keep far out of reach of men; and yet from a vain and forbidden search into the mysteries of our religion, and from determining peremptorily and minutely of what hath been left at large and undetermined in the revelation which God hath given us, almost all the contentions have arose which have disturbed the peace of the Christian Church.'

Yet this opposition to the free play of reason, to speculation which might end in Arianism, made Warner none the readier to plunge into the other current of the time, Evangelicalism, which he called enthusiasm. In effect that meant Methodism, though Warner sometimes used it of dissent in general: the reason why Cromwell had been 'a bad-hearted man' was that 'all his religion . . . was enthusiasm, without any rational or solid principles'. The trouble with the Methodists was that although they followed scripture, they used it selectively. 'No doctrine', he wrote in the *Advice*, 'which is peculiar to the Christian system must be derived from one passage detached from all the rest. To the want of attending to this distinction, and to an absurd way of explaining particular texts, which seem by the sound of the words to speak a sense of their own distinct from all the rest, are owing the wildness and inconsistency of the modern Methodists; and the great disturbance of many serious people, and the destruction of true religion. To the same absurd way of considering and explaining scripture it is owing that our Saviour's short and plain institution, founded in reason, obvious to common sense, and which appeals to the heart and conscience, is defaced and obscured with paradoxes, mysteries and senseless propositions. By grounding their sentiments on obscure texts, or explaining the most obvious ones mysteriously and with allegory, either by interpreting some passages according to the sound of words, or reasoning about the sense of them from their own conceived opinions, they make anything of anything.'

He added in a later letter: 'To preach Christ with them is not to preach Christian morals – how much soever Christ did it himself – but to play off a set of phrases, without ideas and without connection, in which the word Christ is always mentioned; and instead of persuading us to practise the virtues which he taught by his life and doctrines, which is the end of all religion, they recommend only an amorous enthusiastic sort of devotion, in the love of Christ, in faith, and hope in Christ, and phrases of such nature, in disparagement of moral virtue, and in contradiction to his laws.'

These attacks on the Methodists were entirely unfair, given the specific emphasis on holiness in the preaching of their founder, John Wesley. They were also out of keeping with Warner's efforts to be a man of peace. When he thought about it, he deplored controversy. He reminded his Andover hearers that the founder of the faith had recommended 'forbearance, meekness and goodwill'. In the preface to his Prayer Book commentary he said: 'I have taken all the care I could to avoid any uncharitable censures and appellations, as being wholly opposite to the religion and example of our Saviour Christ.' The general tone of his *History* was eirenic. It allowed that in the 1662 split there had been extremists, including bishops, on the Anglican as well as the nonconformist side; and the ejected ministers had suffered hard usage of a kind which 'cannot be remembered without regret'.

Yet his ungrudging regard was kept for the great figures of the Church's centre, like Tillotson – 'the best and greatest archbishop of Canterbury, next to Cranmer, which has ever filled that see'. Warner's tolerance faltered when it came to highchurchmen; and it ran out altogether in face of Roman Catholics. Popery as well as enthusiasm, he found as he finished the *History* in 1759, was making 'terrible advances upon us'. At

Borden, thirty years before, he had displayed a curate's fierceness: the Church of Rome was Antichrist, and its religion 'a real mystery of iniquity'; it allowed people by superstitious rites to reconcile a wicked life with the hope of heaven, it permitted and even required persecution, its clergy were 'luxuriant in vice'. In his *Rational Defence* he claimed that popery 'carries in it everything terrible to Protestants and Englishmen: persecutions, massacres, fire and faggot, miseries and calamities insupportable, not to be described by any pen, must be the inevitable consequences attending it'. As for transubstantiation. the *Free and Necessary Enquiry* maintains that 'the notion was artfully invented, and the belief of it introduced, by the crafty and designing priests of the Church of Rome to aggrandize their power and make them a sort of demi-gods among the people. Wonder, O heavens! and be amazed, O earth! at the stupendous impudence of those priests of Antichrist, who are almost every day making gods innumerable . . .'

He stops short of persecution, but only just. In his last book, a work of Irish history, he grows indignant over 'swarms of Jesuits' filling the kingdom. 'A liberty of conscience to all those who have been born and educated here in that religion is one thing, and God forbid it should be retrenched; but to permit an army of foreign priests to invade us, and to corrupt the minds of Protestant subjects, is another.' He adds, unreassuringly: 'Let me not be misinterpreted. Far be it from me to wish that the Government should go to the length of all the cruel, intolerant statutes of Elizabeth and James I. I mean only such to be put in force, and in the gentlest manner, as would prevent the increase of popery.'

In his human dealings, Warner could be kindly enough. The most notable evidence of that is his long years of work on the idea of an insurance fund for the widows and children of clergymen. It was a concern which went well beyond his own household. He first broached the idea in about 1744, apparently on his own initiative. He spelt out the details in 1752: every clergyman who joined the scheme would pay a fixed sum of about £6 a year, in return for which his widow would be entitled to a pension of up to £20 a year. By 1755, in a further pamphlet, he was proposing varying rates of contribution. He explained the general need: 'The legal maintenance of the clergy being only for their lives, in many cases but a bare competence, in most cases not even that, it does not enable them to leave their families in such a comfortable situation as is commonly done among us by every other degree of men. The clergy are debarred by their profession from any trade or commerce to assist a scanty income; and yet they live, or should live if they are supposed to do any good, above the rank of labourers and mechanics; they should live like gentlemen.'

He returned to the theme in 1759 as a tailpiece to his *History*. Pluralities and non-residence were absolutely necessary now in the Church of England, because of the 'wretched condition' of the ordinary clergy: out of nine thousand or so churches in England and Wales, six thousand did not pay more than £40 a year, and the incumbents could not provide for their families. So he had drawn up a scheme for 'a general annual contribution among ourselves'; clerics 'in almost every part of the kingdom expressed their approbation'; but it 'was not countenanced', he regretted, 'by those who were most called on by their rank and station to support it'; and his attempt to promote a parliamentary Bill had collapsed in the same way.

By 1764, when Warner was honorary president of Sion College for a year and raised the topic yet again in an open letter to the fellows, one or two smaller versions of such a scheme were operating in areas outside London. The duke of Newcastle, nearing the end of his life, now reappears in Warner's story. In October 1763 Warner asked a favour not for himself. 'My Lord, though I could not succeed in my attempt for making a provision for all the poor widows and orphans of the clergy', he wrote of his schemes so far published, 'yet this good has resulted from them, that they have put many dioceses and counties on making some provision in their own particular districts'. One such was the part of Surrey which encompassed both Barnes and the duke's house at Claremont. Warner asked for a subscription to the fund: the great name of Newcastle would of course go to the top of the list of subscribers. Nearly two months went by without a response. Finally a letter bearing the Newcastle seal was delivered to Barnes rectory. Warner opened it in the belief that the new society was to be honoured with the duke's subscription.

The letter contained not a word about the fund. It was a request that Warner should secure his son John's vote for a Whig friend of Newcastle's, Lord Royston, who aspired to an honorific post at Cambridge. John Warner was an M.A. in residence at Trinity. Newcastle had the grace to be a little sheepish, having done nothing for the Warners all these years; but Warner gathered his fallen dignity about him. It was not in the power of neglect or ill usage, he declared, to make him desert his principles. 'My Lord, I cannot help having my feelings; but I am an honest man. As little therefore as my party has done for me, I shall never be found wanting in the day of trial. Accordingly as soon as I received your Grace's letter, I did not hesitate a moment in determining my son's vote for Lord Royston.' And three months later, relying still on his son's easy-going disposition, Warner wrote of a contest for the university high stewardship: 'Your Grace may absolutely depend on my son's vote for Lord Hardwicke.'

Newcastle's gall was the more remarkable because a little earlier, in March 1763, he had done John Warner an active disservice, denying him a City lectureship. The father had entered a momentary protest: 'I thought myself entitled to ask so small a favour as your Grace's directing your steward to interest himself among the parishioners of St Clement's in favour of my son, who is a candidate for that lecture, and whose abilities are not exceeded by any competition. It is therefore a great surprise to me to receive a letter from him this morning, in which he says "The duke of Newcastle has sent round in favour of *Stainsby*".' Was this not cruel usage, Warner had asked the duke. Now in March 1764 he reported that his son was again a loser because of the promised vote for Hardwicke: it brought out the worst in Warner's old patron Surly Bob, now Lord chancellor (who had a different candidate, the earl of Sandwich). 'My Lord chancellor is so enraged that my son's vote is given on that side, as that he has publicly declared he will not give him the living I had asked and he had promised for him in Kent, nor any other.' The Newcastle blight descended equally on father and son. In 1765 Warner was claiming that because of his devotion to his party, 'of which I have ever looked upon your Grace as the head, I have lost a prebend from the Great Seal, and my son a living in Beds of £150 a year which was kept on purpose for him if he had not voted against Lord Sandwich; and the chancellor, it is probable, would have made me a dean, as he did his other chaplain.'

The duke, who returned briefly to office in August 1765 after a period out of it, did at length bestir himself. At the father's instance he gave the son the living of West Ham, on the other side of London, and received him 'in the most handsome manner' – though the living soon turned out 'not so good by £100 a year as we thought it'. John Warner – a good classical scholar who had been at St Paul's school – was a little more fortunate than his father: he became a well-known preacher at a private chapel on Long Acre, in Covent Garden, and then passed by way of a pair of Bedfordshire villages and a particularly rich incumbency in Wiltshire to the chaplaincy at the British embassy in Paris. The Wiltshire post was as rector of Stourton, and it was at least an indirect consequence of Ferdinando Warner's strivings, since it was the gift of a wealthy man whom John Warner knew from Barnes. He was Sir Richard Colt Hoare, of the Fleet Street banking firm; the family had a house at Barnes as well as Stourhead.

But the father's unrecognized state persisted to the last. There was a new pathos in his tone when he wrote to the duke in September 1765, noting that the dean of Windsor and a canon of Christ Church were dead: 'I have lost as much or more than I now ask, besides my son's living, for serving your Grace by his conduct at Cambridge; and therefore with my age and infirmities, and after so many disappointments, if your Grace does not bestow one of these vacancies upon me it will break the heart of your Grace's most obedient humble servant, Ferdo. Warner.'

His son's pretensions and his own, he reminded the duke in December 1765, were 'very distinct things'. Three months later he was asking the duke to press a claim he had made to the last administration for a gratuity in return for the dedication of another book, a *History of Ireland*. 'It is very hard, my Lord, that I should suffer for being a friend to this administration when they were out of power, and when they came into power they should refuse to do me such a favour as to procure me so small a debt from the Crown.'

His last appeal was written in July 1766, when he had discovered that the archdeaconry of Colchester and a prebend of St Paul's were to be vacated by another man's preferment. The two together did not amount – and his old hand wrote the words large to stress them – to one hundred pounds a year. 'The time hath been that if such a favour as these two little things united had been *offered* me by your Grace, as a compensation for my pretensions, I would have *refused it*; and even now, my Lord, if I was a few years younger than I am, I would not *ask it.*'

Yet the most he ever got from all his self-abasement before the duke was a little help with his historical research. Two of Warner's last works, published in the 1760s during his Barnes period, were works of Irish history. The first took the story of Ireland from the earliest legends to 1171 – the date of the earliest English invasion, under Henry II. The second was a *History of the Rebellion and Civil War in Ireland*, which picked up the story merely between the years 1641 and 1660. The duke's contribution was to help Warner establish, to his own satisfaction, that ninth- and tenth-century Danish invaders of Ireland had not carried any Irish records back to Denmark. The duke put the enquiry in the hands of the British ambassador in Copenhagen, who reported that there were no such records in the royal archives there.

The books themselves resulted from Warner's old instinct as a book-maker. He saw a gap in the market: in the course of writing his church *History* he discovered that no good general history of Ireland existed. In the latter part of 1761 he had himself invited to Dublin, where he stayed in Trinity and transcribed other men's manuscript digests of Irish tales and bardic records. But 'it was soon found', he wrote in the preface to the later work, 'that the manuscript materials for Irish history – not to be removed from the places in which they were deposited – were too voluminous to be inspected at the expense of a writer on his own account, or on what might be repaid by the publication of such a work'. An attempt to get financial backing from the House of Commons failed – on the grounds, Warner chose to suppose, that he himself belonged to the party out of power; and he broke off just at the point where England's Irish question began. He selected his two seventeenth-century decades because they showed Roman Catholics in revolt against the State.

His health was by now failing. It was one reason why he was glad to abbreviate the Irish undertaking. His affliction was gout. From 1757 on it had figured increasingly in his letters. 'Even lame and helpless as I have been this winter', he once wrote to Hardwicke, 'I have not forgotten or neglected to vindicate my friends whom I thought unjustly aspersed; as the enclosed pamphlet, which I wrote in bed crippled with the gout, will bear witness.' On another occasion he wrote to the duke in a new, neat, sloping hand: 'My Lord duke, I have not only been unluckily laid up with the gout for some time past, which has prevented my waiting on your Grace as I intended, but it lies so heavy in my right hand that I am not able to make even this application to your Grace but in the handwriting of my son.' (A vicarious twinge of shame crosses the reader's mind, as it must have crossed Newcastle's, lest the father should be making the son his accomplice in a begging letter; but in fact Warner only wants a further historical enquiry set on foot through the British mission in Madrid.)

The gout was the final irony. It was one of the dear duchess's chief afflictions, and Warner made a study of it. In that respect Hume's role as general counsel to the Newcastles could actually have been better discharged by Warner. His last and most likeable book, published in 1768, was about gout. Its aim was humble enough: the whole title was *A full and plain account of the gout; from which will be clearly seen the folly, or the baseness, of all pretenders to the cure of it: in which everything material by the best writers on the subject is taken notice of; and accompanied with some new and important instructions for its relief, which the author's experience in the gout above thirty years hath induced him to impart.* Warner in fact claimed that he had had his first touch of gout at seventeen, which persuaded him that in his sixties he might be able 'to furnish many of his gouty brethren with some few means of relief that have not yet been pointed out'.

Like nearly all Warner's books, it is a compilation, but sieved in this case by his own experience. Much of the book is taken up with ways to make the pain less. He passes on a recipe for laudanum, for example (an ounce of choice opium sliced thin and shaken up with three ounces of distilled rainwater), 'which if the whole College of Physicians were to exclaim against, I will maintain at the peril of my life, if it was required, is as safe as bread and butter'. His pragmatic approach was particularly effective with gout in the fingers (from which the duchess suffered). He was sceptical about poultices, whether made from putrefied elder-flowers or from a mixture of rye meal, yeast and salt; he found burying the affected part in hot sand safer and less trouble. 'By the same sort of remedy somewhat differently applied – sweating it in turf – I recovered the perfect use of a lady's hand, contracted and shut so hard by a fit of the gout as to be deemed, in a consultation of some of the best surgeons in London, impossible to be opened without breaking all her fingers to pieces.'

Warner thanked God for laudanum, and for the fact that gout drove out other disorders. He drank two or three pints of whey every dinner-time, ate only one dish of 'animal food' in a day, and confined himself in the same period to three glasses of wine at most. 'By the blessing of God, and a strict adherence to this regimen, and to other particulars above specified, which are also drawn from my own practice, the gout that was wont to disable me for three or four months in a year doth not confine me now, unless owing to an accident – like composing this account, or some external hurt – above so many weeks in a year. In short, I have no more gout than my constitution hath made necessary to free me from all other bodily ills; and those who know me know that few people at my age, and who have led such a sedentary, studious life as I have, possess a greater share of health and spirits than I enjoy.'

The preface is dated Barnes, October 20, 1767 (when Warner was sixty-four). The book had enough success to warrant a second, or at any rate an Irish, edition, published in Dublin in 1769 for two shillings and eightpence-halfpenny. The new edition added an index, which was useful, but not the information that the author had died in the intervening year. There was evidently some bodily ill from which gout had not protected him at the last. It may perhaps have been a broken heart.

5 'The author of society'
(1758-1863)

A LIFE SPENT BATTLING AGAINST INFIDELITY, POPERY
and enthusiasm turned out to have been a life wasted. As the
eighteenth century gave way to the nineteenth, they all
continued to flourish – and not only outside the Church of
England, but inside. It was bound to happen. If you translated
Warner's trio as reliance on human reason, reliance on tradition
and reliance on scripture, they represented just those forces which
Anglicanism existed to hold in balance; and movements of
thought at the time kept them all vigorous.

Take the play of reason first. When Hare and Warner
discounted the deists – the men who found the existence of God
reasonable, but not the divinity of Jesus – they reckoned without
the European common market in ideas. The English deists
became an influence in Germany. So did Voltaire, the most
trenchant of their French fellow-travellers. It was in the
atmosphere thus created in German universities that scholars
first felt able to apply normal critical methods to the Bible,
asking who the authors were and what human causes made them
write as they did. That spirit of instructed scepticism returned
to plague English nineteenth-century believers.

Devotees of tradition, next – both Roman Catholics and their
Anglo-Catholic sympathizers within the established Church –
took an extra strength from political accidents. In 1800 Pitt the
younger brought the whole of Ireland into the United Kingdom
– which thus found itself with about a quarter of its population
Roman Catholic. Political discrimination against Catholics
became increasingly hard to justify, and in the Catholic
Emancipation Act of 1829 they were at last allowed to become

MPs and hold public office. (Many nonconformist disabilities were being lifted at the same time.) The impulse behind Pitt's Act of Union was the anxiety to prevent Ireland's being used as a staging-post for an attack on England by post-revolutionary France. Within Anglicanism, the French revolution had another consequence. Many of the English devout, perceiving the fall of the French national Church and the fact that the ideas of Voltaire had something to do with it, were frightened that the Church of England would go the same way if modernism in religion and politics were given its head. That partly explained the counter-attack of the traditionalists under the banner of the Oxford Movement (or Tractarianism, as it was nicknamed from the tracts which made it known).

The biblicism of enthusiasts or Evangelicals, finally, took on something of the quality of a second Reformation; and the old faith it rebelled against was precisely the religion which Hume and Warner had accepted without question, and which had discovered a fourth person of the Trinity in the duke of Newcastle. Great numbers of Evangelicals nevertheless remained within the accommodating arms of Anglicanism. Some of them did become Methodists; but John Wesley died an Anglican, and although by 1795 Wesleyan Methodism was a separate Church, its departure was the last great schism which Anglicanism suffered. Alongside Tractarianism, the Evangelical revival was to become part of a great renewing wind through the Church of England in the nineteenth century.

Of these three voices, the first, free enquiry, was remarkable for being not much heard at the parish level; and that silence persisted and became hallowed. The search for truth was recognized as being a dangerous business. If Barnes heard little of the achievements of biblical scholarship, the same was true of parish congregations all over England. The other two movements, Evangelicalism and Tractarianism, each had its notable representative in Barnes, one after the other: Henry Melvill and Peter Medd. Between Warner and Melvill came four men who represented their age in other ways.

The first of the four was Christopher Wilson, rector of Barnes between 1768 and 1792, and for the last nine of those years bishop of Bristol as well. His few surviving sermons are elegantly garnished with scriptural allusion; but his approach was a world away from the biblicist fervour of the Evangelicals. Submission to God was a matter of cool logic. The observer could perceive that the uniformity of nature, the regular returns of day and of the seasons, 'are in reality the never-ceasing exertions of the same supreme power which gave birth to its existence, and without which it must immediately fall back into chaos'. That is from a 1785 sermon in Westminster Abbey: it was the argument from God the cosmic watchmaker much used in William Paley's *Evidences of Christianity* nine years later.

Wilson's chief interest in that line of reasoning was as an exhortation against social disorder. The divine designer wanted the same orderliness in his human creation: 'government itself is the ordinance of God'. For the subject, it was partly a matter of self-interest: if he knew his place, his rulers would have no occasion to encroach on his liberty. 'Let all parties join their endeavours to repress the universal spirit of licentiousness which seems to have overflowed the whole nation and levelled the bounds of every order and distinction', Wilson concluded. 'Let every man submit himself to the established laws of society, as the institution of the author of society.' (One can see why the lawyer Sir William Blackstone, after hearing all the celebrated preachers in London at about this time, declared that 'not one of the sermons contained more Christianity than the writings of Cicero'.)

Wilson was in fact a careerist and pluralist in the old mould – as if determined that his century should keep its character to the end. He even owed a couple of early steps up the ladder – it comes as no surprise – to the ageing Newcastle. Wilson was well connected: his father was recorder of Leeds, and he was a friend of the marquis of Rockingham. He was an undergraduate and then a don at St Catherine's, Cambridge: towards the end of his time there he was both vicar of a nearby village, Coton, and a university proctor. He left Cambridge to become a prebendary of St Paul's and then of Westminster Abbey. He married a daughter of Bishop Gibson of London, a stern old high-churchman who denounced court masquerades and preached a sermon – Warner borrowed it – in favour 'of temperance in eating and drinking'. The Newcastle influence was instrumental at this point in Wilson's becoming a chaplain to the king and a canon of St Paul's: he wrote to Newcastle from the Abbey in June 1758 to make 'the most sincere acknowledgments of my great obligations to your Grace for this fresh instance of your goodness in recommending me to His Majesty's favour'. At this stage Wilson gave up his Westminster prebend, but not the St Paul's one. Barnes was then added through the influence of the St Paul's chapter, and the bishopric of Bristol through the Rockingham connection. For the last nine years of his life he was thus possessed of four jobs; and he died several miles from any of them, in his house off Berkeley Square.

He was buried with his father-in-law and his wife in the churchyard of All Saints, Fulham, the church at the northern end of Putney Bridge which stands at the gates of Fulham Palace, then the home of the bishops of London. (He is commemorated inside the church, at the base of the huge medieval tower, in an ornate marble monument which gets his own and his wife's date of death wrong.) He was thus more permanently in the neighbourhood of his Barnes parishioners than he had ever been in life: most of the entries in the church registers during his quarter-century as rector are signed by a curate. Still, the *Gentleman's Magazine* (never one to knock the great) claimed in 1788 that Wilson preached at Barnes most Sundays; and he was in the district often enough to meet an antiquary named Daniel Lysons, who was curate of Mortlake in the 1780s and Putney in the 1790s. At Putney Lysons began work on his big book, the *Environs of London*; and when he came to write about Barnes, early in the next century, his recollection of the former rector was full of a curate's gratification at having been spoken to by a bishop. 'Dr Wilson was a man of very amiable manners', Lysons remembered, 'and had the good fortune of conciliating general esteem. Steady and uniform, though not violent, in his political principles, he enjoyed not only the respect, but the friendship, of those who differed from him in opinion. When elevated to the bench, through the interest of his deceased friend the marquis of Rockingham, he took the surest

Christopher Wilson

method of making the Church to which he belonged, and its rulers, respected and esteemed, by maintaining the strictest discipline, at the same time that he behaved with the most unbounded affability to persons of every rank and description, particularly the inferior clergy.'

It was under Wilson that there began a process familiar in the eighteenth and nineteenth centuries: the expansion of the parish church building beyond its medieval shell. Until now, Barnes church had consisted for three hundred years of a single nave with a square tower at the west end – the archetypal English parish church. Previous rectors had done no more than tinker with it: Warner had had the inside whitewashed. But Wilson himself was at a vestry meeting in 1777 to propose that a leading parishioner should have leave to take down part of the north wall and add a three-tier private chapel of his own: a gallery for his family, a ground-level pew for his servants and a vault for his dead. (The parishioner was Sir Richard Hoare, father of the Hoare who helped John Warner.) Nine years later this excrescence was enlarged into a complete second aisle.

The process was continued under Wilson's two successors, a father and son both called John Jeffreys. Jeffreys senior, rector only from 1792 to 1795, grappled with dry rot and embellished the tower with a clock and a sundial: the sundial bore some of the words addressed uncomprehendingly to Jesus by two of the disciples at the end of the road to Emmaeus – 'Abide with us, for the day is far spent.' Jeffreys junior had the church 'painted, coloured and whitewashed' in 1813; installed more seats in 1818; and replaced the old barrel organ with a new pump organ in 1829. A London journalist, William Hone, commented sourly in an 1832 miscellany: 'The church of Barnes, an antique structure, has had its interior modernized by the despoilers, misnomered "beautified".' Undeterred, Jeffreys junior extended the second aisle again in 1838.

The problem to which all this expansion was addressed was not a rise in the number of churchgoers. The time of revival was not yet. Indeed, Jeffreys senior found church attendance so low that he devised a system of using two local charitable funds as bribes: 'he thought', says a vestry minute, 'that it would tend

Barnes church from the south-east, 1818

to the greater advantage of the poor, and promote their attendance at church, if the produce of the funds were given away in bread at the church every Sunday, and at Christmas day and Good Friday, but to such persons only who shall duly attend divine service.' Nor was the local population increasing. As late as 1843 the *Illustrated London News*, although conceding that Barnes was 'rife with interesting associations', reported: 'The place consists of a few straggling houses opposite a common, of a mean street leading to the riverside, and of a row of elegant houses facing the Thames on a broad terrace nearly half a mile long.' The clue to all this church expansion seems to have been financial. In an age when pews were still rented, the church was in a position to sell social standing to families who could afford higher rents than their neighbours; but if there were to be these profitable gradations in pews there must be plenty of pews.

That apart, the Jeffreyses were a pair without history. They were descended from the youngest and clerical brother of Judge Jeffreys, the hanging Lord chief justice of the last of the Stuarts. They were both at Christ Church, Oxford. Jeffreys senior was a barrister's son: he figured as a small boy, along with a tame duck, in an open-air family group by Hogarth. Grown to manhood, and besides holding other minor cures, he was rector of Berkhamsted in Hertfordshire from 1756 till his death, and a canon of St Paul's from 1779. As such he was able to secure the living of Barnes for himself when Wilson died; but he contrived to transmit it almost at once to his twenty-four-year-old son, and died three years later. Jeffreys junior, too, had other preoccupations: for a while he was also rector of Friern Barnet, just north of London, and he was a chaplain to the Prince Regent. But at Barnes, at any rate, he was not an absentee (a boast which, in the 1820s, six thousand out of ten thousand of the parish clergy could not make). His spell of forty-four years at the rectory remains by far the longest in the church's history. His wife, the daughter of a captain in the Coldstreams, gallantly bore him six sons and seven daughters: when he died, he left the parish £333. 6. 8d in three per cent consols, which was used for Sunday schools; and he lies buried in his own churchyard, near the door of his vestry. (His placid example was contagious: one of his

The Jeffreys family

sons, after a spell as curate under John Keble at Hursley in Hampshire, was vicar of Hawkhurst in Kent for fifty-eight years.)

He was succeeded in 1840 by a man whose surname is familiar in nineteenth-century Anglican history, Reginald Copleston. There was a new flurry about expansion, as the road which led from Barnes to Hammersmith Bridge through orchards and market-gardens began to have houses built along it: first there was a chapel of ease for the new settlement, then there was talk of demolishing the parish church and rebuilding it altogether, and the temporary solution which Copleston adopted was to enlarge the second aisle yet again. This 1852 renovation was beneficent: much of the in-filling and plastering and whitewashing done by Warner and the younger Jeffreys in the original aisle was removed, disclosing medieval roof-timbers and the thirteenth-century lancet window at the east end. The problem about the sheep without a shepherd on the road to the bridge was met in the 1860s by a new church at the river end.

Reginald Copleston arrived as a young man, like his predecessor, and stayed twenty-three years. (He served fifteen years after that at Edmonton, north-east of London.) He came, by way of Exeter College, Oxford, from an old and wealthy Devon family. Enough of its wealth adhered to him to allow him and his wife to keep half a dozen servants at Barnes rectory, including a footman, a lady's maid, a nurse and a nursery maid. It was also a clerical family: his grandfather, his father and his elder brother were all successively vicars of Offwell in Devon. Another brother had a Gloucestershire rectory, and two sons born at Barnes became colonial bishops.

But Reginald's most notable connection was his uncle, Edward Copleston – provost of Oriel, Oxford, dean of Chester during his last Oriel years, and then (between 1828 and 1849) concurrently bishop of Llandaff and dean of St Paul's. Bishop Copleston prided himself on not using his patronage for the benefit of his numerous clerical relatives; but as dean of St Paul's at the time he will at the very least have known that a nephew was being appointed to Barnes (even if the appointment was made by another member of the chapter), and may

Barnes rectory from the south, 1823

there fore be supposed to have found his nephew's views roughly in line with his own.

Although Edward Copleston was one of the last of English bishops to wear a special episcopal wig, he passed among his peers for a liberal. He supported Catholic emancipation, not on the grounds that Catholics deserved it but in the sophisticated belief that to remove their sense of persecution would be to deprive them of their reasons for obstinacy in error. He was similarly for easing the remaining problems of nonconformists. Keble and John Henry Newman, founders of the high-church Oxford Movement, were fellows of his college under him; yet he deplored their work. In face of their opposition he successfully backed, first for the Regius professorship of divinity at Oxford and then for the bishopric of Hereford, an Oriel man (Renn Dickson Hampden) who argued that the creeds of the Church were of human rather than divine origin.

It may well be that Reginald Copleston sympathized with some of these attitudes in his uncle the dean. But there is no sign that they were preached to his flock. They were the stuff of discourse in lecture-rooms, not parish pulpits. David Friedrich Strauss's *Life of Jesus* – the work in which the legacy of the eighteenth-century English deists returned from Germany to England, marking the beginning of modern divinity – was published in an anonymous English translation in 1846, during the Copleston years at Barnes. (The translation was by Marian Evans, before she became George Eliot.) Strauss contended that although Jesus was recognizably a moral genius, his story had been encrusted with myth made by the first Christian communities. If that had been preached at Barnes, some trace of the resulting fracas would have survived. There is no such trace. Of the ideas which moved through nineteenth-century Anglicanism, that was not one which interested the mass of the clergy. But Evangelicalism and Tractarianism – despite the forbidding names, here were causes to quicken the blood.

6 'War with the devil' (1812-1871)

THE JEFFREYSES FATHER AND SON, AND REGINALD Copleston, were a trio who left few footprints. But the next incumbent at Barnes, Henry Melvill, documented his life and even his era exhaustively. He represents, with considerable accuracy, the movement which was changing Anglicanism and England during the Jeffreys-Copleston period, the first half of the nineteenth century. That movement was Evangelicalism.

The Evangelical movement was nothing less than an attempt to improve the morals of a nation; and it had a certain success. Its central tenet was that the cause of vice was unbelief: diminish the second, and you would diminish the first. It developed, within the established Church, the religion of the heart which Wesley had rediscovered; but it also showed a worldly-wisdom, and therefore an effectiveness, which escaped Wesley altogether. Piety, prudery, philanthropy, imperialism – all the attitudes which most notably characterized the Victorian mind came direct from the Evangelicals. It is one of the most important movements of opinion in the history of Anglicanism, and it survives still.

Henry Melvill was in the middle of it. He was born, at the end of the eighteenth century, into a family which was among its earliest adherents. Through his family he knew all its founders and leaders. He worked with many of them. His life's work was as a preacher; and he became in the 1830s a popular preacher, and in the 1850s the leading preacher of his day. The hundreds of sermons he left behind are remarkably pure and clear evidence of the quality of Evangelical thought. Historians of Evangelicalism have neglected him unwisely.

Even before we reach his sermons, the story of his life is a
guided tour of the dearest Evangelical principles. Evangelicals
believed, first of all, in conversion; and Melvill's father, a
Scottish infantry officer, was converted, and saw to it that his
children were laid open to the same experience. Conversion was
the moment – it might be instantaneous, it might be long-
drawn – when in Melvill's later words a man was 'super-
naturally excited to a war with the devil'. By the grace of God,
he recognized the great things done for him through Christ and
felt bound to attempt great things in return. Only then could he
call himself a 'religious' or 'serious' man, professing a 'genuine'
or 'sincere' or 'vital' Christianity. Indeed, since no nineteenth-
century churchman acknowledged being a party man or liked
using party labels, and since Evangelicals were especially coy in
that regard, those adjectives became their code words for 'on
our side'.

The means to the conversion of Henry Melvill's father Philip
was a volume of Cowper, the movement's poet, pressed into his
hands during his long convalescence from near-fatal wounds
sustained in India under Warren Hastings. Philip Melvill later
became lieutenant-governor of Pendennis Castle, overlooking
Falmouth harbour, a Tudor fortress which he had remarked as
a 'desirable residence' on his first landfall from India; and there
he brought up his children. He and his friends regarded both
survival and posting as signs of divine intervention in his favour.
It was an honour Evangelicals were prone to claim.

Not all his children lived to adulthood; but Evangelicals
valued deathbeds. 'It is a beautiful thing to see a Christian die',
Henry Melvill said: 'he who can be present, and gather no
assurance that death is fettered and manacled, even whilst
grasping the believer, must be either inaccessible to moral
evidence, or insensible to the most heart-touching appeal.' He
had first taken this lesson in at the age of no more than five,
when an eleven-year-old brother was 'seized with a rapid
decline' (in the words of a memoir of the father). 'His piety,
resignation and heavenly-mindedness from the beginning to the
end could not be surpassed; in prospect of death, he attempted
to console his parents who were almost overwhelmed with grief,

and in a sweet yet solemn manner reproved his elder brother for wasting time in the perusal of light and trifling books.'

The deathbed reproof must have had its effect. Five years later the elder brother, now a subaltern in the Gunners, was drowned on a boat-trip off Madeira; and the Melvills felt sufficiently confident that he had died converted to ship out a tombstone which recorded at its foot their 'joyful hope of meeting him again in the regions of bliss, through an interest in HIM who loves his people with more than a father's love, even *Jesus Christ*, whom to know is life eternal. Reader! Know that nothing short of an interest in *Christ* can save thee from the wrath to come and bring thee to everlasting life.'

An 'interest' in Christ was an Evangelical speciality. It was not on a level with an interest in shell-collecting or astronomy: this was the kind of interest one had in a limited company – a stake, a share in the equity, an indefeasible property right. Salvation was an offer with which one closed. A popular Evangelical hymn of Philip Doddridge's about conversion ('O happy day that fixed my choice') referred to it baldly as a transaction. Evangelicalism well understood that it could not reform the nation without support from men of substance; and it spoke to them in their own tongue.

It was a family faith. Prayer and Bible reading at home, and especially in the family group, were its staple. Philip Melvill put his children through a systematic course. 'He made it a rule to open the instructions of the day with an appropriate prayer, in which his children reverently joined. Religious reading always formed a part of the daily course of instruction, and Saturday was regarded exclusively as a day of preparation for the Sabbath. On this day, therefore, he carefully catechized his children, questioned them on scriptural subjects, remarked on the faults they had committed during the week, with a close application to their understandings and consciences; and noticed with approbation and kindness what was commendable in their behaviour.'

Sabbatarianism was an Evangelical passion. Here, thirty years before Victoria, was the genesis of the Victorian Sunday. 'His children were exhorted to rejoice with him in having

another Sabbath to enjoy', the sympathetic memoirist remembered. 'Upon this sacred day, he lectured his children, before
they went to public worship, on some important religious
subject, suited to their capacities and feelings, which had
engaged his thoughts and pen on the preceding evening. During
the intervals of service (too often wasted by young people in
indolent vacuity of mind), the elder children were required to
commit their thoughts to writing on the same subject, and were
constantly questioned respecting what they had heard in the
sermons of the day. Early rising throughout the year was the
invariable practice of the whole family. Thus time was gained
to every member of it for religious reading before breakfast,
and it was expected that the children should recite some passage of scripture at the breakfast-table, quoting chapter and
verse.'

Henry Melvill learnt the lesson for good. The Sabbath, he
told Cambridge undergraduates thirty years later, is 'the rent
we pay God for our lives'; and fifteen years after that he was
explaining to a City lunch-time audience why it was a mistake
to open your shop on a Sunday, even if that was your busiest
day.

(The explanation came in a form he often used as a clausula
for each separate part of a sermon; he would start with an
exclamation, and end with a return to his text. 'Oh, the
waverer between duty and interest may point out to us how the
sustenance of his household apparently depends on the traffic
which we entreat him to renounce, and he may speak pathe-
tically of the penury which threatens to come in like an armed
man, if he listens to our advice – but we have only one thing to
say against all this dwelling on present advantage; and that one
thing is not in depreciation of the boat and the net, but simply
what our Lord said to Peter: "Every one that hath forsaken
houses, or brethren, or sisters, or children, or lands, for my
name's sake, shall receive a hundredfold, and shall inherit
everlasting life".')

Young Henry Melvill was so far from rebelling against the
strenuous piety of his upbringing that by the time he was
thirteen he had already begun preaching, and with his father's

sergeants to practice on. 'Morning and evening devotions were never omitted in his family. The regular course was a portion of scripture, with practical remarks from Henry, and prayer. Visitors were informed of the family custom, and invited to join it. Non-commissioned officers and others in attendance for orders were likewise called in.'

The great Evangelical instrument for practical reform was the society. There were societies for every conceivable object: punishing the wicked, protecting the morally endangered, converting the faithless, distributing wholesome literature, prosecuting unwholesome. Philip Melvill was active in the Naval and Military Bible Society (founded in 1780) and the British and Foreign Bible Society (founded in 1804). He planned another charitable institution, a clothes fund, 'with a view to procure and encourage the regular attendance at church of such destitute poor (in large towns probably not a few) as from the want of decent clothing unwillingly absent themselves from the house of God'. There were to be proper safeguards. The chosen poor were to be issued with their church clothes on Saturday night, and were to hand them in again on Monday mornings: only after steady attendance on several Sundays could they keep the clothes for good. But before he could add this newcomer to the swollen roll of Evangelical societies, the governor was called to his own reward.

Evangelicals stuck together. That memoir of Philip Melvill, compiled by an anonymous friend of the same persuasion, was published in 1812 on subscription: an adequate number of readers had to put themselves down for an adequate number of copies before a group of sympathetic publishers (led by Hatchard's of Piccadilly) would take the book on. But Evangelicals were indefatigable joiners: the book came out with a list of subscribers at the back that reads like a roll-call of the Evangelical high command. William Wilberforce took two copies – the wealthy Yorkshire MP, remembered chiefly for his campaign against slaving, who led the movement for nearly forty years. Zachary Macaulay was in the list – Thomas Babington Macaulay's father; so were all the other Evangelical families who, living near Wilberforce at Clapham, became known as the Clapham Sect – Babingtons, Barclays (the brewers), Elliotts, Grants, Thorntons. So was Hannah More, moralizing novelist, and Harriet Bowdler, sermon-writing sister of the man who disembowelled Shakespeare and Gibbon so that they could no longer 'raise a blush on the cheek of modest innocence nor plant a pang in the heart of the devout Christian'. So was Henry Hoare, head of the banking house (and half-brother and heir of Sir Richard Colt Hoare of Barnes): so were numbers of company directors, MPs, senior officers, clergymen and Cambridge dons. Henry Melvill was thirteen when his father died. It was in this world that he was reared.

Six years later, in 1817, he went up to St John's, Cambridge, as a sizar. Cambridge has always sheltered the low-church interest (as Oxford has the high-church): home of the Puritans in the seventeenth century, it was a centre for Evangelicals in the nineteenth. St John's was a particular refuge, and remained so: in Samuel Butler's autobiographical (and hostile) account of Evangelical undergraduates at Cambridge forty years later, in chapter forty-seven of *The Way of All Flesh*, he says that their headquarters were at Caius 'and among the sizars of St John's'. Even then they were still called Sims, which was short for Simeonites, after the widely influential figure who had been vicar of Holy Trinity church at Cambridge for fifty-three years to 1836 – Charles Simeon. Melvill was an original Sim. He was up in Simeon's time, thought him 'a great and good man', and after he had left Cambridge came back at Simeon's request to preach for Simeon's favourite cause, the Society for the Conversion of the Jews. (There were no bounds to reforming Evangelical optimism just then.)

Melvill was one of the two best mathematicians of his year. It was still not possible to read theology as such at Oxford or Cambridge: theological studies were mixed in with classical and scientific, to furnish the equipment of the Christian gentleman. But once Melvill had become a don at Peterhouse his childhood bent for preaching reasserted itself. He might have remained a university pulpiteer; but after about seven years a familiar problem presented itself. He wanted to get married; and that meant giving up his fellowship and his livelihood.

The Evangelical connection came to his rescue. It was a practice among Evangelicals to advance their brand of church-manship, and thence (they hoped) the cause of national good behaviour, by using their money. One method they favoured was the setting up of proprietary chapels – Anglican churches privately owned by individuals and trusts that could then appoint the minister. These chapels were not parish churches, and they were reluctantly tolerated by the episcopate because they supplied the shortage of churches in newly built areas without necessitating the trouble of drawing new parishes. There was one such at Camberwell, in south London, called the Camden chapel. (The surviving local tradition is that it was set up when the parish church, St Giles, began showing dangerous signs of high-churchmanship by having two candles on the altar.) The chapel's leading trustee was Henry Kemble, a businessman and MP, one of three brothers whose names recur on the committees of endless reforming societies. Kemble had heard of Melvill, and now invited him to become the chapel's incumbent. Melvill subsequently dedicated a volume of sermons to Kemble and another brother 'in acknowledgment of many acts of kindness which it is pleasing to commemorate but impossible to requite'; and Kemble married one of Melvill's sisters. Evangelicals were assiduous intermarriers.

Belonging to no parish, a proprietary chapel was chiefly a preaching-station. For Melvill, the move was the entry on his life's work. He took the highest possible view of preaching. He perceived already that he had the gift of holding an audience. He knew, certainly, that the actual impact might not be as great as the apparent. 'It is a melancholy and dispiriting thing', he said in a sermon dating from his Camden period, the 1830s, 'to observe how little effect seems wrought by preaching. We take the case of a crowded sanctuary where the business of listening goes on with a more than common abstraction. We may have before us the rich exhibition of an apparently riveted attention; and the breathless stillness of a multitude shall give witness how they are hanging on the lips of the speaker. And if he grow impassioned, and pour out his oratory on things terribly sublime, the countenance of hundreds shall betray a

convulsion of spirit – and if he speak glowingly of what is tender
and beautiful, the sunniness in many eyes shall testify to their
feeling an emotion of delightsomeness. But we are not to be
carried away by the charms of this spectacle. We know too
thoroughly that with the closing of the sermon may come the
breaking of the spell; and that it is of all things the most
possible that, if we pursued to their homes these earnest
listeners, we should find no proof that impression had been made
by the enunciated truths, and, perhaps, no more influential
remembrance of the discourse by whose power they had been
borne completely away than if they had sat fascinated by the
loveliness of a melody, or awestruck at the thunderings of an
avalanche.'

He knew, further, from his own experience up to that time,
that preaching entailed a risk to the preacher – that he might
become as bored as a tourist guide. 'No one', he told his
Camberwell congregation, 'whose profession it has been, for any
length of time, to act the part of a spiritual guide, can be other
than his own witness to the fact that there is the very greatest
likelihood of his coming to view with a languid and uninterested
eye the glorious things which he has to exhibit and explain; of
his acquiring a fluent and effective phraseology which shall
paint to others the several parts of the moral panorama and
convey, it may be, to the hearer a most accurate idea of the
harmonies and the splendours which pervade the infinite circle,
and yet being all the while as void of an actual feeling of the
preciousness of the redemption wrought out by Christ, as if it
were rather a tale to be illustrated by an ingenious lecturer than
a fact to be laid hold on by the perishing sinner.'

It remained true, Melvill believed, that preaching was God's
ordinance. 'The ordained preacher', he proclaimed, 'is a
messenger, a messenger from the God of the whole earth. His
mental capacity may be weak – that is nothing. His speech may
be contemptible – that is nothing. His knowledge may be
circumscribed – we say not, that is nothing; but we say, that
whatever the man's qualifications, he should rest upon his
office.' The public ministrations of the word, he told his hearers
at Great St Mary's on one of his returns to Cambridge, 'are the

instituted method by which the events of one age are to be kept fresh through every other'. The sermon, therefore, was nothing less than the designated instrument to conversion and ultimately to salvation – or to damnation, if its message went unheeded; and there was a moral beauty in the occasion, which lay simply in the fact 'that the gathering to the house of prayer, and the listening eagerly to the word, may be taken as proofs that men feel themselves immortal, and long to learn how heaven may be gained'.

For Melvill, they began to gather in considerable numbers. By 1839 Henry Crabb Robinson, *Times* man and diarist, was describing him as 'the popular preacher' – and finding him, at a dinner-party, 'cheerful and agreeable, and not at all puritanical'. On Sundays the conductors of horse-buses starting for Camberwell would call out Melvill's name as the star attraction of the route. The crowded congregations were evidence of Melvill's gifts, in voice and language. They also showed that the Evangelical revival of those years was no mere product of organization: it corresponded to a real stirring of opinion. Great numbers of men and women were bored by the idleness and self-seeking of the established Church and yet wished to remain within it.

In 1840 Melvill's talents were noticed by the duke of Wellington himself. On the strength of a speech he heard Melvill make, the old duke had him appointed chaplain to the Tower of London; and to lessen his ducal discomfort at having to sit through an annual sermon at Trinity House, he arranged that Melvill should deliver it. Wellington was about as unconverted a figure as could well be found; but Evangelicals, from Wilberforce down, perfectly understood the importance of winning the support of the people that mattered.

They took trouble, too, to see that their own men filled key posts. Since the beginning of the century they had had their men in high places in the East India Company, which they valued for its missionary potential. One of them was James Melvill, Henry's elder brother: he became the Company's secretary. But they had little hold over the establishment where the Company's officials were trained for Indian service – a college for young men

Henry Melvill

of undergraduate age at Haileybury, near Hertford. Late in 1843 the college principal resigned. His deputy, James Jeremie, was a clergyman, but by no means an Evangelical: he conspicuously lacked the Evangelical capacity for hard work. Melvill, meanwhile, found himself worn out with preaching. 'Under the severe strain upon his powers, physical as well as mental,' relates his own anonymous memoirist, 'his health at last gave way so far as to induce him to accept the offer made to him by the directors of the East India Company to take the office of principal of their college at Haileybury.'

The move was in interesting contrast to the later pattern, when tired headmasters retreated to pulpits; and Melvill's promised repose was impaired by bad relations with his deputy, who resented being passed over. They continued till Jeremie left six years later for Cambridge, where he caused continuing comment by combining the Regius professorship of theology with the deanery of Lincoln and doing the duties of neither. But with Melvill's appointment the college became an increasingly serious place; and he himself continued the practice of bringing in sound men by appointing, to teach history and political economy, Sir James Stephen.

Stephen was a Colonial Office permanent secretary who had retired early, and a founder member of the Clapham Sect. He carried the Evangelical suspicion of pleasure to the point of caricature. 'He once smoked a cigar,' his son Leslie wrote of him, 'and found it so delicious that he never smoked again.'

It was a puritan trait, and the streak of puritanism in the Evangelicals was strong. Melvill was by no means extreme in this respect, as Crabb Robinson had noted. Like other Evangelicals, he said surprisingly little against the evils of drink: several leading figures among the converted were after all brewers. But he was strong against the corrupting effects of pleasure, not least intellectual pleasure. There is an occasion in Acts (at 19.19) where a number of Ephesians are stimulated by St Paul's preaching to burn a load of books; and in a sermon published just before he came to Haileybury, Melvill was all for extending the practice to modern literature. 'How numerous the works of an infidel tendency!' he cried. 'How yet more numerous those of an immoral! What a shoal of poems and tales which, though not justly falling under either of these descriptions, can but emasculate the mind of the reader, filling it with fancies and follies, and unfitting it for high thought and solemn investigation!' Incalculable viciousness was fostered by 'loose but beautiful' verse. Melvill then catechized the converted on a wider range of pleasures. 'You found that worldly amusements – the theatre, with its licentious accompaniments; the masquerade and the dance, with their frivolity, at least, if not their sinfulness; the card-table, with its trial of temper, even where it did not excite the spirit of gambling – you found that these warred against the soul, whilst you were yet unconverted; but what have you done as a proof and result of conversion?'

He was a kindly enough man, and with a kindly enough wife, to yield one point to his new charges when he found how short of diversion their Hertfordshire solitude left them. He gave evening parties; and at these parties – the recollection comes from a colleague, an orientalist named Monier-Williams – 'dancing was not an unusual incident'. But Melvill was at one with mainstream Evangelicalism in a distrust of the intellect, or of the pursuit of any truths except truths relating to salvation.

Another part of Melvill's equipment for his Haileybury post was an unquestioning imperialism. Evangelicals believed Britain to be the new Israel, charged to show the purposes of God to the world at large. That was the justification of empire: that was why, in a May 1859 sermon in St Paul's Cathedral, Melvill took it for granted that the suppression of the Indian Mutiny was arranged by God and a matter for thanksgiving to him. 'Throughout the fourteen years', he then said reminiscently, 'during which I had the honour and the happiness to preside over the education of the civil service of India, a service which has done gloriously in the recent mutiny, I did not fail to tell the young men entrusted to my care that it would not indeed be their place as servants of the Indian Government to preach Christianity, but that, nevertheless, they ought to be as missionaries to the Hindus and the Mussulmen. I have told them that though they were not to preach Christianity, they were to live Christianity, recommending it by showing how it produces finer morals, loftier and purer motives, less selfish and more generous actions than are found amongst the slaves of error and superstition. This I told them was their mission, as splendid an one, oh, far more splendid than chivalry has ever assigned its favourite champions. In ways such as these, we trust, will much be done towards putting the weight of the governing body on the side of our holy religion. But we have also our part to do. India is open to our missionaries, and we shall altogether fail in our duty, our thanksgiving will be nothing better than a mockery, if we do not make every effort to cover the land with faithful preachers of the gospel of Christ. There is nothing but this gospel which can raise India from its degradation.'

The young gentlemen were not always receptive. In Monier-Williams's recollection, Melvill was not at his best in Haileybury chapel. 'He always seemed, when there, to preach in fetters, or perhaps I should rather say to be hampered by a consciousness that his peculiar style of eloquence was more adapted to a general congregation than to a college chapel. No doubt even the most experienced preacher might well feel embarrassment at seeing before him a number of self-sufficient youths – most of them wise in their own conceits – who prided themselves on despising all emotional appeals to their higher natures, and were disposed to regard every sermon, however eloquent, as a something to be tolerated on the principle of unavoidable acquiescence in a necessary affliction.'

Monier-Williams also found Melvill short on decisiveness and tact. But the college had always been difficult to administer. So far from choosing his own students, the principal had them chosen for him. They were nominated by members of the East India Company's court of directors. The college was the gateway to a vastly lucrative career: Indian civil servants made fortunes. The directors therefore chose their nominees from among their own and their friends' families, and expected Haileybury to pass them out without fuss. So dismissal, as a stick to wave at the idle and to use on the incapable, was simply not in the principal's cupboard; and standards of work and discipline suffered.

Melvill seems not to have greatly minded. He found the

directors 'gracious and considerate masters', and would have been prepared to see the system continue. It was in fact doomed even before he went to Haileybury: Parliament was beginning to comb out the country's grosser inefficiencies. In the early 1850s, Melvill sat on a Government commission of inquiry into the choice and training of Indian civil servants. Among the other members were Thomas Babington Macaulay and Benjamin Jowett, the Balliol don – both of them men who had been brought up in the Evangelical fold and left it. Macaulay largely wrote the commission's report: it found in favour of open competition, on an agreed syllabus, between young men from any place of learning. There would be no further need for a special one. The Government accepted the report. At the end of 1857 the era of the 'competition-wallahs' began, and the college closed (though it opened again five years later as a public school). Melvill's speech at the last rites went as near as he could towards saying that the change was for the worse.

He was himself of sufficient fame as a preacher not to lack work, though he never attained the kind of church dignity which his eminence laid claim to. That was a common experience for Evangelicals, then and later: their numbers on the ground were not matched by their numbers on the bench of bishops. Melvill was by now considered the greatest pulpit performer of his day. Among his admirers was Gladstone: he told Canon William Sinclair of St Paul's that he 'never heard any who kept the attention of his hearers so closely'. Melvill had maintained his reputation while he was out at Haileybury by delivering Tuesday lunch-time sermons to City workers at St Margaret's, Lothbury. They were called lectures, and they paid £400 a year: endowing lectureships which their own men could fill was another Evangelical recourse. His sermons were published, admired and copied: at least once, on holiday in the Lake District, he found himself sitting through one of his own. He was pirated in an ill-printed weekly called the *Pulpit*, which reprinted single sermons in double columns and in countless Evangelical households was the nearest thing to Sunday entertainment on offer. His fame reached higher: while he was

Barnes church from the south-east, 1869

still at Haileybury he became a chaplain to Queen Victoria, who had Evangelical leanings. Yet, with all this, the summit of his attainment – it came to him from Palmerston as a consolation for the collapse of Haileybury round him – was a canonry at St Paul's.

He never complained. He was no Warner. In that respect he genuinely possessed the 'humility of mind' which his memoirist (in a few pages at the front of his last sermons) identified as his chief characteristic. Preaching the word was his appointed task, and it was enough. And to his canonry he was able to add, on Copleston's going in 1863, the rectory of Barnes. Not merely was it a St Paul's living: it had colourable Evangelical connections through the Hoares and another leading Evangelical family, the Venns. Melvill moved to Barnes rectory, with wife and daughters, for the last seven years of his active life.

He was by now sixty-five. He used old sermons a little more often than in former years; but he took his new parochial responsibilities seriously. Barnes was expanding: there were new villas on the London side, and a growing area of workmen's housing up river towards Mortlake. Melvill launched an appeal for a new church in each neighbourhood, contributed liberally to it himself, and established a school-room church in the Mortlake direction. At Camberwell he had provided religious instruction for the children of the congregation, and sometimes visited the sick: now that he had a proper parish, he could not do less.

He was struck, during these parish rounds, by the weakness of the dying: if they were not already converted, they had very little strength left for 'labouring after an entrance into the heavenly inheritance'. It would be helpful for the unconverted, he said in one of the sermons of this period, to accompany him on these visits. They would see the danger of leaving their change of life until too late.

It is impossible to know whether he died in the assurance he had urged so many others towards. He fell seriously ill in 1869, and resigned his Barnes post in September 1870. He was still a canon of St Paul's, and for a while he tried to resume his duties there; but he was too weak. Partisanship, at any rate, was by now far from his thoughts. A new canon had just been appointed, Henry Liddon, a leader of the opposite wing of the Church from Melvill's. He sat by Melvill's bedside a good deal; and Melvill confided to another acquaintance: 'I have liked and admired many men, but I never *loved* any man as I do Liddon.'

He died early in February 1871. The inscription on his gravestone in the floor of the cathedral crypt concludes: 'He lived the devoted minister of Christ, the earnest preacher of the word of God. He died resting all his hope on the assurance of that faithful saying: "Christ Jesus came into the world to save sinners".' Melvill had chosen that final text himself.

He had lately come to believe – as had many Evangelicals, during a new revival of their fortunes in the 1860s – that a second coming of Christ would not be long delayed, and that the dead would somehow rise physically from the grave to see it: 'Come the magnificence of descent, the pomp of judicature, the renovation of the earth, the grave shall not hide these wonders from our view.' Some forty years later the body of Sir William Howard Russell, war correspondent for *The Times*, was laid on one side of Melvill's, and of Sir Lawrence Alma-Tadema, painter of vast crowd scenes in magnificent settings, on the other. Melvill would have thought the group providentially brought together: if these were the right men to record the event, in words and pictures, he was certainly the man to make sure that the appropriate lessons were drawn. He had preached about it often enough.

What, in essence, was the Evangelical message? It was that Christianity – so long as it was serious, and genuine, and vital; in other words, Evangelical – could make men good. Christianity was, in Melvill's phrase, 'the great civilizer of manners, the great heightener of morals'. There is a passage in a sermon of Melvill's, dating from early in Victoria's reign, which reads like an Evangelical manifesto. His text was the saying of Jesus (at Matthew 10.34) about bringing not peace but a sword. The sword had occasionally been wielded against each other by Christians, he conceded – mostly by papists; but from now on optimism was in order (a pre-twentieth-century optimism). 'It

is easy to upbraid our religion, because it hath fulfilled its own
prophecies, and proved itself a sword; but what engine has been
so efficient as this sword in accomplishing results which every.
lover of virtue admires and every friend of humanity applauds?
What hath banished gross vices from the open stage on which
they once walked unblushingly, and forced them, where it failed
to exterminate, to hide themselves in the shades of a disgraceful
privacy? We reply, the sword Christianity. What hath covered
lands with buildings unknown in earlier and much-vaunted
days, with hospitals, and infirmaries, and asylums? We answer,
the sword Christianity. What is gradually extirpating slavery
from the earth, and bringing on a season, too long delayed
indeed, but our approaches to which distance incalculably those
of the best heathen times, when man shall own universally a
brother in man, and dash off every fetter which cruelty hath
forged and cupidity fastened? We answer unhesitatingly, the
sword Christianity. What hath softened the horrors of war,
rendering comparatively unheard of the massacre of the
unoffending and the oppression of captives? What hath raised
the female sex from the degraded position which they still
occupy in the lands of a false faith? What hath introduced laws
which shield the weakest from injury, protect the widow in her
loneliness, and secure his rights to the orphan? What hath given
sacredness to every domestic relation, to the ties which bind
together the husband and the wife, the parent and the child, the
master and the servant; and thus brought those virtues to our
firesides, the exile of which takes all music from that beautiful
word *home*? To all such questions we have but one reply, the
sword Christianity.' Christianity had lifted our fallen humanity
'to a moral greatness which seemed wholly out of reach'.

How had these Evangelical triumphs been won; how were
they to be maintained? In plain terms, by frightening people
with hellfire. That was the importance of the last judgment. 'It
must be true of every one of us', Melvill said at Camberwell,
'that he cannot take a step which is not a step nearer to the
judgment-seat, not one which is a step further from his accuser.
Would that this might be considered by you all! Would that
this of itself might suffice to force on you the thinking in what

degree you are prepared for the unavoidable trial! Oh, surely
it is not overrating the power of the simple representation, if we
believe that the most careless and irreligious in this mass would
be awed into something like seriousness, or moved to something
of alarm, were he to set himself for awhile to ponder the facts –
"I am always on my road to a judge who must condemn me on
sufficiency of evidence; and I have always at my side an accuser
whose charges are too plain to dispute.' "

This accuser, noting every sin, was God; the judge was Jesus;
and the judgment was to happen, for everybody, at the end of
the world. 'There is to come, as you well know,' he told
Camberwell for its seasonal comfort one Christmas eve, 'a day
when the whole population of this globe, from Adam downwards
to the latest of his kind, shall be put upon trial, and receive
sentence according to the things done in the body.' Until then
the souls of the dead were simply to wait, either in confidence or
foreboding. And the sentence would be an eternal stretch in
heaven or hell – a city 'ineffably beautiful', or a place of
'unutterable torments'. All this was determined by one's stay on
earth: 'heaven begins now or never, upon earth or nowhere.'

But this was a more subtle exercise than merely luring people
with rewards and frightening them with punishments. If you
were 'awed into something like seriousness', you were in a fair
way to lay hold of the central truth of the faith, which was that
redemption could be had through Christ. 'There, my poor
friend, is the way to be saved', Melvill said in St Paul's in 1859:
'go to Christ for everything. You want strength to enable you to
forsake what is bad? Go to Christ for the strength. You want to
repent of your sins? Go to Christ to make you repent. You want
to have faith in Christ? Go to Christ to give you faith. You want
to be able to pray? Pray to Christ that you may pray. Do not
fancy you are to get on as far as you can by yourself, and then
turn to Christ when you can get no further. The first thing is to
go to Christ, the last thing is to go to Christ.' If you followed
those instructions, and were met with grace, then you were
converted. If you were converted, you would go in the end to
heaven: those who repented and believed were assured of a
place there. For that very reason, though, you would try your

hardest to be good on earth; it was the least you could do in return. Even so, you would not be good enough to deserve heaven: that would be impossible – it would be justification by works, which was heresy; but you would be better than you would have been otherwise. 'In the very proportion in which the notion has been discarded of works availing to justification,' he told one of his City lunch-time throngs, 'have works been wrought as evidence and effects of justification.' The strongest faith was habitually accompanied by the warmest love. The duties of the converted life – prayer, Bible-reading, church-going, scrutiny each evening 'of what we have been throughout the day' – would be a further help. It was by that process that sin would diminish as infidelity did.

Yet that picture of a heaven where not everybody went sat uneasily with another cherished Evangelical notion: the idea of an all-seeing, all-loving providence. 'I believe of this providence', Melvill said in St Paul's, 'that it encircles alike the palace and the cottage, guiding and upholding alike the poor and the rich, ministering to the king in his counsels, to the soldier on the battlefield, to the scholar in his study, and to the labourer in his husbandry; so that whatever my rank and whatever my occupation, at no moment can I be withdrawn from the eye of God, in no lawful endeavour am I left to myself, in no secret anxiety have I only my own heart with which I may commune.' This divine vigilance attached to 'those whose heart is perfect towards God' in particular. 'We are believers in the doctrine of the universal providence of God', Melvill went on; 'and we believe, further, of this providence, that the great object which it proposes is the stability and exaltation of Christ's Church.'

Indeed, this was a belief much voiced by Evangelicals from the first. Simeon saw the finger of God in a succession of accidents which altered the balance of a Cambridge committee meeting in his favour. Wilberforce believed that God deliberately delayed the moment of his conversion until after the election which first took him to Parliament. Once converted, he said, he could not 'have adopted the methods by which I ingratiated myself in the goodwill of some of my chief supporters'. He must have meant bribery; and he must further have meant

that God intended the bribery, in order to get himself a 'serious'
MP.

The difficulty about providence was this. If God's control of
the minutiae of human affairs was as close as that, then it was by
God's decision that some people became converted and others
did not. That would mean that he doomed certain people to
hell before they had even done anything to deserve it – which
was exactly the reformer John Calvin's position. Melvill was an
even more reluctant Calvinist than Calvin. He fell back on
declaring the problem a mystery. We had scriptural warrant
for believing that God elected certain people (to hell as well as
heaven, though Melvill could not bring himself to be as explicit
as that), and we had scriptural warrant for believing in man's
free will. 'But how can these apparently opposite statements be
reconciled? I know not. The Bible tells me not. But because I
cannot be wise beyond what is written, God forbid that I should
refuse to be wise up to what is written. Scripture reveals, but it
does not reconcile, the two. What then? I receive both, and I
preach both; God's election, and man's free agency. But I
should esteem it of all presumptions the boldest to attempt
explanation of the co-existence.' He took what comfort he
could from the line in Revelation (at 7.9) about a multitude
which no man could number. It did at least show heaven to be a
place of 'vast capacity'.

The great convenience of the Evangelical doctrine of providence was that it wiped out, at a stroke, the problem of evil.
Everything was meant. Why should rain fall on the just as well
as the unjust? Because God intended it. There was very little
difficulty, of course, about the unjust: they brought their
suffering on themselves, either as a divine retribution for their
sin, or as a natural consequence of it, or as an expression of the
general truth that all human suffering followed from the first sin
of Adam. As for the sorrows of the just, the awkwardness disappeared if suffering was seen as a form of teaching. They
were 'trained for immortality' by bereavement, made 'fit for
heaven' by pain, permitted to serve as a guide to others by the
fortitude with which they bore a lingering death. 'When you
observe how express are the assertions of scripture as to the

unwillingness of God to apportion pain to his creatures, you must allow that suffering is permitted because nothing but suffering will suffice.'

Yet Melvill was severe on the notion – lamentably often encountered by the parish minister, it seemed – that suffering sufficed by itself. It was not a ticket to heaven, for all that was said about consolations hereafter. 'A life of misery is no security against an eternity of torment.' Other proofs of piety were needed besides: notably, conversion.

It was hard on the poor; but then, much of Evangelicalism was hard on the poor. Wilberforce and his friends had realized from the start of their long campaign that they had no hope of reforming a whole nation unless they had on their side the support, and therefore the example, of its ruling class. (One of the movement's earliest and most influential tracts was one published by Hannah More in 1788. It was called *Thoughts on the Importance of the Manners of the Great to General Society*.) If you wanted the rich on your side, you could have no truck with political radicalism – especially when the red glare of revolution was still visible across the Channel. Wilberforce was in fact much criticized for toiling to abolish slavery overseas – the British slave trade was prohibited in 1807, and slaves in the British West Indies were freed during the 1830s – while showing no interest in analogous wretchedness at home. As an Evangelical attitude, it seems to have persisted. In *Bleak House* – the 1853 novel in which Dickens is almost as hard on Evangelicals as he is on lawyers – Mrs Jellyby is so taken up with 'telescopic philanthropy', so busy with plans for the cultivation of coffee by the natives of Borrioboola-Gha on the Niger, that she has no time to deliver her own children from dirt and neglect. Yet Wilberforce was more consistent than his critics allowed. He abominated slavery not because it denied people liberty but because it withheld from them the opportunity to hear and follow the gospel. His interest was not philanthropic but missionary. The thraldom of the London poor, however, or of the Irish peasantry, was merely economic: they had plenty of opportunity to hear the word preached if they cared to go and listen. And beyond that Wilberforce's interest did not extend.

Melvill shared in this social quietism to the full. Radicalism
was unscriptural: enough said. He was not sure, he said from his
Camberwell pulpit in 1835, 'whether there be not something of a
necessary alliance between democracy and irreligion'; and he
added, warming to his work, that infidelity and anarchy went
hand in hand, and scepticism and sedition were twin brothers.
(The sermon was attacked by one of his own parishioners in an
indignant pamphlet.) Melvill's line never changed. His published
preaching spanned a period from 1833 to 1870 – exactly
Dickens's writing life as a novelist; and from start to finish it
showed absolutely no concern to change the condition of the
poor as Dickens so unanswerably documented it. For them, as
for everyone else, the important thing was their welfare in
another world than this. The Christian should relieve actual
destitution on his doorstep; but he need be in no doubt that God
meant the poor to be poor. 'We hold it to be clear to every
student of scripture', Melvill said in his earliest volume of
sermons, 'that God hath ordained successive ranks in human
society, and that uniformity of earthly allotment was never
contemplated by his providence.' (Exactly the same point was
more graphically put in the notorious verse of 'All things bright
and beautiful', published in 1848, which declared: 'The rich
man in his castle, The poor man at his gate – God made them
high or lowly And ordered their estate.' The young woman who
wrote that – she became Mrs Alexander – was an Evangelical
at the time. She later softened in her views and withdrew the
verse.)

God had nevertheless not overlooked the poor, Melvill
maintained. The psalmist was quite right in contending (at
Psalm 68.10) that God had prepared for them of his goodness.
There was after all enough food to go round: if some people did
not get enough, that was human mismanagement, not divine.
Further, Christ died for the poor as much as for the
rich; the truths of scripture were as available to the unlearned
as the learned. In fact, they were more available, because the
'village Christian' (a figure to whom Melvill, with his university
and urban ministry, can have been little exposed) was peculiarly
well armoured against modern scepticism. 'We believe of many

a village Christian, who has never read a line on the evidences of Christianity, and whose whole theology is drawn from the Bible itself, that he would be to the full as staunch in withstanding the emissaries of scepticism as the mightiest and best-equipped of our learned divines; and that if he could give no answer to his assailant whilst urging his chronological and historical objections, yet by falling back on his own experience, and entrenching himself within the manifestations of truth which have been made to his own conscience, he would escape the giving harbourage for one instant to a suspicion that Christianity is a fable.'

That was the other main arm of Melvill's conservatism: doctrinal; and its basis was the Bible. Whatever scripture said was right. 'The Bible is throughout to be implicitly depended on', said Melvill from Camberwell, 'as neither recording historically anything but facts, nor delivering didactically anything but truths.' The reason for this reliability was that all its various books had a single author, and that author divine. 'The Bible comes to us' – Melvill used this sentiment on two separate occasions during the 1850s – 'as the dictate of one mind, and the writing of one pen.' The claim that this mind and pen were God's was self-authenticating. Melvill had said in Cambridge twenty years before: 'Evidences of the divine origin of the Bible press themselves quickly on the most illiterate student, when he searches it in humility'. It therefore followed that the rules about birds'-nesting in Deuteronomy (22.6, 7) were divinely ordained and still binding; that Elijah did go up to heaven in a chariot, that Jonah was swallowed and regurgitated by a whale, and that Herod did slaughter the innocents, pointless though the whole exercise might seem to have been. Melvill spent a whole sermon finding merit in the unattractive little detail in Revelation (at 22.5) that in the heavenly Jerusalem there was to be no night. Indeed, he could claim that the basis for all his certainties about heaven and hell was solidly scriptural. Awkward, mutually contradictory passages? 'Difficulties there are in the Bible', he blandly conceded to the undergraduates in Peterhouse chapel; 'but they ought rather to assure, than to make you doubtful of, the divinity of its origin.'

What defeated a human understanding was all the likelier to spring from a divine. There could be no faith, in Melvill's view, without total faith in the Bible; but that was enough. 'We require nothing', he said, 'but an admission of the truth of scripture'. Fundamentalism was fundamental.

Encased in this Protestant confidence, Melvill was able to take a short way with dissentients, whether they were Roman Catholics, biblical scholars, or scientists. Roman Catholics had a new freedom to press their case after George IV, sobbing, had signed their emancipation into law in 1829. In the following decade the success of the Oxford Movement marked a strengthening of Anglicanism's Catholic arm which was without parallel since Laud; and actual defections to Rome, notably Newman's in 1845, became common events. So low-churchmen like Melvill could hardly help approaching the struggle to keep the Church of England one Church with a renewed polemicism. England had been (in Melvill's view in 1850) 'honoured by the Almighty as no other land hath been', as the repository first of Protestantism and then of that empire which might disseminate it; yet the heritage was in danger. The 'nominal Christianity' among Anglicans against which Evangelicals always inveighed – and which they now especially detected in high Anglicans – was little better than Roman Catholicism, 'for whenever formality has insinuated itself into religion, or self-righteousness, or the substitution of means for an end, then has there been introduced the very essence of Romanism'; and as though this were not enough, 'have we not, of late years, as a nation, ay, and even as a Church, tampered with popery?' The reference was to the decision the same year that Roman Catholics might have their own bishops, and to increasingly ritualistic services in certain Anglican churches. 'A heavy responsibleness rests on our land, as being the land where there was fought a great battle between error and truth', he said in St Paul's in 1859, as if the Reformation had been an entirely English affair: 'God grant that we never lose sight of this responsibleness'; and he felt sufficiently strongly to fish the same passage out of a drawer for a sermon of his Barnes period.

His own case against Roman Catholics was, naturally.

scriptural. Like all his views, it remained unchanged throughout
his working life. 'Ours', he roundly declared in a sermon from
the early 1830s, 'is the old religion; theirs is the new. Ours is, at
least, as old as the Bible; for it has not a single tenet which we
do not prove from the Bible. But theirs must be younger than
the Bible; for where in the Bible is the Bible said to be insufficient,
and where is the Pope declared supreme and infallible, and
where is sin divided into mortal and venial, and where are the
clergy forbidden to marry, and where are images directed to be
worshipped, and where is the Church entrusted with the
granting indulgences? There is not a solitary article of Protestantism in support of which we are not ready to appeal to the
canonical scriptures, and the writings of the early fathers; there
are hundreds of popery, which papists themselves are too wise to
rest on such an appeal.'

He wavered from scripture for one moment, when he flirted –
in defence of the same point about the antiquity of Protestantism – with a beguiling folly then current among scholars.
'Whatever may be thought', he said carefully, 'of the opinion
which has been supported with great learning and ability, that
St Paul himself preached the gospel in Britain, and ordained a
bishop here before there was any in Rome; so that the Anglican
Church would be older than the Roman; it is, at least, certain
that Christianity made its way into these islands at a very early
period . . .'

It was Melvill's only nod to contemporary scholarship. The
rest he deplored. The deists he baldly equated with Cain. 'Cain
was the first deist', he told a Cambridge audience in 1839: 'the
first man who held that reason was sufficient for man's guidance,
and that all professed revelation might be rejected as un-
necessary.' But the deists had a powerful new heir in Strauss,
the man who explained away the supernatural elements in the
gospels as myth, arising after Jesus's lifetime among followers
who expected a Messiah to have performed miracles and fulfilled
prophecies. Melvill must have heard of Strauss. He nevertheless
responded only by pouring general scorn on sceptics. It was
enough for him that claims by Jesus to divinity were recorded in
St John's gospel. Either these things were said untruthfully,

Melvill argued, in which case the survival of Christianity was inexplicable; or they were said truthfully. He never addressed himself to the third possibility, that they were not said at all.

When Strauss was published in English in the 1840s, nothing much happened at first. In nearly every Anglican pulpit, the growing body of biblical scholarship was simply ignored. By the middle 1850s, this silence had become troubling to two Anglican divines in particular. One of them was Jowett of Balliol (a lapsed Evangelical like George Eliot, Strauss's translator); the other was Frederick Temple, a future archbishop of Canterbury. They were instrumental in putting together a book of papers by seven hands called *Essays and Reviews*. It came out in 1860. Its governing idea was that Christians ought not to be afraid of new truth. The validity of their faith did not depend on the accuracy of a detailed chronicle, nor on miracles and fulfilled prophecy: it was known by its moral impact. The Bible, Jowett suggested, should be read in the same educatedly critical spirit as any other book.

The consequent outcry ended in prosecutions for heresy which were finally thrown out by the Privy Council. Again, Melvill did not disturb his congregations at St Paul's or Barnes with direct notice of the book; but he did at one point concede that the truths of scripture might be metaphorical rather than literal. Even then his old instincts reasserted themselves. One of his last sermons was about Saul's visit to the witch of Endor (in I Chronicles). At one point he acknowledged that the narrative was 'abrupt and obscure'. Not for him, though, the kind of explanation which was already becoming available: that two hands were at work, that the author had not understood his source, that the text was corrupt. He preferred to believe that the obscurity was deliberate – 'God probably designing to prevent the prying too narrowly into mysteries so unhallowed'.

Besides biblical scholarship, the other wedge slowly being driven between the intelligent believer and simple faith was the work of scientists. At the beginning of Melvill's preaching life, just before Victoria's reign began, the growth science was geology. Rock strata, fossils, traces of pterodactyls, all began to suggest that the account of creation in Genesis could not hold –

a world made in six days, and (on the accepted calculation from
scripture) in 4004 BC. Theologians fell slowly back on the
thought that, even so, the hand of God could still be detected.
But Charles Darwin's biological work on evolution by natural
selection, published in 1859 in *The Origin of Species*, suggested
that the marvellous complexity of nature might arise more from
chance than divine design.

Melvill knew of this body of work. At Great St Mary's in 1836
he was still maintaining that 'we are indebted to the Bible for
all our knowledge of the early history of the world, of the
creation of man, and of his first condition and actions'. But in
1838 he published a sermon which nodded to the new discoveries. 'There has been much anxiety felt in modern times',
he wrote, 'by the supporters of revelation, on account of alleged
discoveries in science, which apparently contradict the Mosaic
record of the creation. We had been accustomed to conclude,
with the Bible for our guide, that this globe was not quite six
thousand years old; that, six thousand years ago, the matter of
which it was composed was not in existence, much less was it the
home of animal or vegetable life. We had been accustomed to
think that, unless man had fallen, there would have been no
decay and no death in this creation, so that every beast of the
field would have walked in immortal strength, and every tree of
the forest waved in immortal verdure. But modern science is
quite counter to these our suppositions and conclusions: for the
researches of the geologist oblige us to assign millions, rather
than thousands, of years as the age of this globe, and to allow it
to have been tenanted by successive tribes of living things long
before the time when man was summoned into being.'

Melvill acknowledged that these findings were conclusive. It
was of no avail to shut one's eyes to the progress of science.
Nevertheless, 'Science may scale new heights, and explore new
depths; but she shall bring back nothing from her daring and
successful excursions which will not, when rightly understood,
yield a fresh tribute of testimony to the Bible.' And he went on to
rehearse a theory that although scripture might not contain the
whole truth, it carried no actual untruth. 'We would adopt the
statement which has been increasingly adopted and supported

by our divines, that the two first verses of the book of Genesis have no immediate connection with those that follow': in other words, that the first day of creation could be as long as you like. As for the notion that 'animals die because man was disobedient', Melvill was prepared to jettison it as not directly scriptural anyway, and not convenient either, since the scale on which they ate each other made it hard to suppose that any of them had once been meant to live for ever.

Further than that, though, from the picture of an all-creating, all-caring providence, Melvill was not prepared to depart. In the same volume he wrote: 'I do not believe it the result of properties which, once imparted, operate of themselves, that vegetation goes forward, and verdure mantles the earth: I rather believe that Deity is busy with every seed that is cast into the ground, and that it is through his immediate agency that every leaf opens, and every flower blooms.' Melvill was inoculating himself against Darwinism even while Darwin was sorting the specimens he brought home with him in the Beagle.

As an unshaken biblicist, it was Melvill's style in the pulpit to take a text in his mouth and worry the last drop of instruction out of it. He would first explain it in its context, and then apply it to the lives of his hearers in half a dozen different ways, clinching each separate application with a reiteration of the text. Part of his vast success as a preacher came, undoubtedly, from his biblicism. Even as you read his sermons now, his total, self-abandoning reliance on the Bible as revealing the mind of God, if we could only read it right, is cumulatively very impressive. Total faith is always impressive. (Later in the century a friend asked the Unitarian philosopher James Martineau why he went to hear the conservative Baptist Charles Spurgeon: Martineau didn't believe that stuff, did he? 'No,' said Martineau: 'but he does.')

Another reason for Melvill's hold over his audiences was his pictorial language. It was not for nothing that he knew and admired Macaulay. He wrote in images. They never crowded so fast into his mind as when his subject was the last judgment. 'Will ye go with me in thought to the august tribunal', he invited a churchful of mesmerized undergraduates, 'and take note of the trials? There is a young man brought before the judge: he died in his prime, the victim of his passions ... A change passes on the scene: it is an old man at the bar; and the accusation against him is that he was wholly negligent of those whom God gave into his keeping ... And now there are many placed together at the bar, men and women: they are accused of giving no heed to the gospel, of neglecting the "great salvation" provided by Christ ... But change the scene again – there is a solitary prisoner at the bar: he is arraigned for the neglect, or unfaithful discharge, of the high duties of a Christian pastor. Are there any to give evidence? Oh, they are well-remembered faces which he sees pressing from the crowd: numbers of his constant hearers ... Then down to the lowest depths of misery and shame, thou careless shepherd ...'

He had fittingly reproachful eyes under bushy hair parted near the middle; he preached in a white knotted stock surmounting a voluminous black gown; and to his graphic style was added a powerfully musical and modulated delivery. 'I once heard him contrast "the angels in heaven" with "the devils in hell" ', a student of Melvill's, Lesley Probyn, remembered. 'It was in a voice which I can only describe by saying that the sound of the spoken words was in perfect harmony with the ideas, and would almost have expressed them to a person ignorant of the language.'

The passage Probyn remembered may well have been this, which Melvill used at least twice: 'It must always be felt as one of the most touching, heart-sickening things, in the scriptural delineation of the day of judgment, that angels, good angels, guardian angels, it may be – the very beings who have watched with indescribable eagerness for some token of repentance, who would have rejoiced with ineffable gladness over the returning prodigal – that these should be the beings destined to "bind up the tares in bundles for the burning". Less terrible would it be, to be delivered over at once to the fierce and malignant, the dark and scowling spirits, who have all along been bent on our destruction, than thus to pass through the hands of bright and gentle creatures – creatures who would have aided us in laying

hold on everlasting life; and whose look of sadness, as they
execute their dread ministry, shall call up immeasurably more
of remorse and self-reproach than the wild triumphant glare of
fiends exulting in their prey.'

Built up of rhythmic periods like that, Melvill's sermons were
naturally long. 'This is our last remark', he would cry com-
fortingly, or 'This is the last thing I have to say', when he was
still five or six minutes out from home. He spoke fast, as if to
cram as much in as he could, and with a rising urgency, until he
came thudding down each time on his text. Monier-Williams
records: 'I can remember that in the early period of his
popularity his sermons often lasted for a full hour or even more;
yet the attention of his congregation never appeared to flag for a
single instant. Even in the largest churches of London crowded
with eager listeners, men, women and children appeared to
hang upon his lips in breathless silence. Not a sound broke the
stillness but that of the preacher's earnest voice penetrating to
the furthest corners of the building. It was Henry Melvill's
habit to pause for a moment or two at the end of the spirit-
stirring perorations with which he was wont to close each
division of his argument, and it was curious to note that whenever the expected pauses occurred, the pent-up coughs and
colds – due perhaps to some long spell of wintry weather –
seemed to be suddenly let loose, till a fresh burst of eloquence
swept away, as it were, all such temporary interruptions and
made every absorbed listener forget his ailments.' These
coughing-pauses fell at the moments when Melvill had come
home to his text; and at the last of them he seemed to fling it,
drained of all meaning, at his congregation's feet.

To fill a big church is no small achievement. Melvill would
not have drawn that kind of crowd if Evangelicalism, the
movement of which he was a potent voice, had not been a
remarkable moral force. Its influence on Victorian life and
thought was dominant: a number of its attitudes survive, a little
shamefacedly, to this day. Yet its support began to fall away
after about 1870 (though Melvill did not live to see the decline);
and even before then it suffered more significant losses. It is
notable how many of the greatest Victorians – not merely

Macaulay and Jowett and George Eliot but the Brontes, Elizabeth Barrett Browning, Charles Kingsley, Ruskin, Peel, Gladstone, Manning, Newman – were reared in Evangelicalism and could not persist in it. Mark Pattison, another defector, was a little severe when he spoke of 'the helpless imbecility of Evangelical writing and preaching' – or Sydney Smith when he described the whole of Evangelicalism, inside and outside the established Church, as 'one general conspiracy against common sense'. But there was a quality in Evangelicalism which, when not positively anti-intellectual, was certainly unintellectual. It was negligent of needed change, both in doctrine and in society. It was smug. The great Victorian novelists gave it a rough handling. Almost the only sympathetic Evangelical divine in their work is Mr Tryan in *Janet's Repentance* (the last of George Eliot's *Scenes of Clerical Life*). Over against him stand Mr Brocklehurst in *Jane Eyre* (a sanctimonious oppressor of children, drawn from life); Mr Chadband in *Bleak House* ('a large yellow man, with a fat smile, and a general appearance of having a good deal of train oil in his system'); Mr Honeyman in *The Newcomes*, who cries into a scented handkerchief during his own sermons; and Mr Slope, exuding a cold, clammy perspiration, in *Barchester Towers*. They are a persuasively odious quartet.

Melvill's crown as the most eminent preacher of his day passed to the new canon of St Paul's, Liddon. But Liddon was a high-churchman, appointed by a high-church prime minister, Gladstone; and Liddon's sermons are still in the second-hand bookshops in great quantities, which means that within living memory they were on many people's shelves – whereas Melvill's, for all their circulation in his lifetime, now have to be sought diligently. Whatever the Evangelicals' spiritual force, the intellectual staying-power was with their high-church competitors, the Tractarians. It was to these that the moral leadership of the Church of England – and the rectory of Barnes – now passed.

7 'My high and sacred duty' (1848-1908)

WHEN A ST PAUL'S LIVING FALLS VACANT, THE DEAN and the four canons take it in turns to choose the new man. At Melvill's death the appointment fell to Liddon; and he sent to Barnes a fellow high-churchman, an Oxford don named Peter Goldsmith Medd. The Church of England at large was discovering that the simplest way to avoid schism was to tolerate wide divergences of doctrine and churchmanship; the worshippers in an individual parish had to learn to do the same.

Medd became a high-churchman, as Melvill had become a low-churchman, by upbringing and education. Mid-century high-churchmanship had a tinge of gentle birth about it; and Medd's father was a surgeon from Leyburn in Wensleydale who had married a Miss Goldsmith of Leyburn Hall – where Medd himself was born. The surgeon bought a practice in Stockport: Medd and his five younger brothers were brought up in one of the town's best houses, winsomely half-timbered. (He was a precocious child. Issued by his father at the age of five with a blank-verse ode on divine providence to learn by heart by next day as a punishment for not having been ready for afternoon school in time, he was standing up in his crib that same evening, book under arm, clamouring to be heard.) His rare youthful diversions, as entered in his 'Life's Record' – a childhood present from his Goldsmith godfather which he kept filled in throughout his life – were balls and shooting-parties and.Lake District or Highland tours. The spiritual home of high-churchmanship was Oxford; and Medd, after three years' preparation at King's College, London, went up as a scholar of eighteen to University College, Oxford, in 1848. It was to be his home for twenty-two years.

The Oxford Movement, as ordinarily dated, was already over. It began in 1833 with an assize sermon of Keble's; it ended in 1845 when Newman, its effective leader, crossed to Rome. Its central principle was that the Church of England was a divine institution. Keble was angry that laymen should have interfered with it (when the post-Reform-Act Parliament, reasonably enough, cut back the superfluity of bishops in Ireland). Newman defected because he came to believe, on the evidence of superior holiness, that the Church of Rome had developed into a diviner institution still. But his defection was not the end of high-church revival. For much of the 1830s, Newman had been the most influential figure in Oxford; and when Medd went up in the late 1840s, there can have been few of the younger dons who had not been touched by Newmans' teaching. Tractarians, in plain fact, regretted the Reformation. But by the mercy of God, they reflected, the English Church had survived it with two precious possessions intact: its priesthood, handed down from the apostles, and its Prayer Book, derived from the beliefs and practices of the undivided Church. It was this brand of faith which Medd embraced.

He was not at first a zealot, though he wore the eager and slightly ingenuous expression of which he kept a trace all his life. 'Taught to swim by old Hounslow at Parson's Pleasure': the Life's Record notes nothing else for his first summer term. The dean of his college, to whom he became attached, was Arthur Penrhyn Stanley, later dean of Westminster; and Stanley counted at Oxford as a liberal. But among Medd's friends at Oxford were Liddon (two years ahead of him at Christ Church, where Edward Pusey – Tractarianism's leader since Newman – was a powerful anchoritic presence) and Edward King (a contemporary at Oriel, later a notably high-church bishop of Lincoln, whose chapel-going was so punctilious as to worry even the head of his own college). Medd himself, as a young man tending towards ordination, compiled two fat manuscript books of private devotions – one in Latin, bound in brown leather, one in English and blue velvet. The brown volume has at the foot of the title-page in Latin 'God be merciful to me a sinner', and goes on through some four hundred double-column pages of Latin prayers, hymns and litanies, closely written in red and black. The English volume has a sequence of 'Short prayers to be committed to perfect memory' for use at recurrent moments, some of them priestly – on first awaking, after dressing, on entering church, on kneeling down, before saying service, at putting on the surplice, at putting on the stole ('Lord, give me grace to bear thy yoke . . .'); and, among much else, a penitential office and half a dozen litanies, including one of Lancelot Andrewes's. The Tractarians especially admired those early-seventeenth-century divines who had pulled the Church of England's centre of gravity back from a reformed towards a Romanist position.

At the end of 1852 Medd was elected a fellow of his college; early in 1853 he was ordained deacon by Bishop Samuel Wilberforce of Oxford. The bishop was another refugee from an Evangelical upbringing. A son of William Wilberforce, he had nevertheless become a high-churchman. Yet he retained a hint of his father's sinuousness: he was beginning to be known as Soapy Sam. Medd stoutly regarded him as 'the greatest of modern English bishops'.

'Took Huntingford's duty at Littlemore', the Life's Record notes that November: it was the village outside Oxford where Newman had established a semi-monastic community some ten years before. The following spring Medd was staying there to help paint the reredos. When Wilberforce opened a high-church theological college at Cuddesdon, across the road from his palace, Medd sang in the choir for the first service. Liddon was the college's vice-principal – though after five years Wilberforce had to let him go to save the college from too great an appearance of partisanship.

Medd began to exhibit the outward signs of Tractarianism. He sported what Evangelicals called 'mark-of-the-Beast' waist-coats (from their similarity to Roman Catholic wear: they buttoned to the adam's apple). Bald as a young man, with only a spot of hair on the top of his head, he wore a great deal of hair on his lower cheekbones: extravagant whiskers were a Cuddesdon mannerism which Wilberforce found it necessary to trim. More privately, as King and Pusey did, Medd mortified the flesh. The practice sometimes got out of hand; 'caught a chill bathing in an ice stream', the Life's Record notes of a journey to the Swiss Alps, 'and travelled home with a sort of dysentery. Ill afterwards at Oxford from this.'

But his dominant Tractarian interest remained the purification of Anglican worship by the revival of old forms. These came from neglected entries in the Prayer Book of 1662, and from its forerunners. In the late 1850s he compiled, and had privately printed, a booklet called *The Priest to the Altar, or aids to the devout celebration of Holy Communion, chiefly after the ancient English use of Sarum* (the medieval modification of the Roman rite which provided the main material for the first book of Common Prayer in 1549). In 1864 he published, with Wilberforce's blessing, a small volume called *Household Prayer*, with suitable material and instructions for its use. ('The congregation should range themselves down the two sides of the room', it suggested. 'The males and females may take opposite sides, or the family one side and the servants the other.') A colleague and friend of his in the University College senior common-room was William Bright, the church historian, who wrote the fine communion hymn 'And now, O Father, mindful of the love': together, the following year, they put the 1662 Prayer Book back into Latin.

(The two of them were well-trained classicists. In a Swiss diligence they once argued Church history for three hours with two Capuchin monks in Latin; and in Pusey's rooms at Christ Church they discussed doctrine with a visiting patriarch of the Orthodox Church in ancient Greek. 'At first the archbishop's pronunciation was difficult to follow,' Medd recalled, 'but the ear soon became accustomed to it.')

The Tractarians were concerned about the way the Church was governed. Parliament was still its rule-maker; yet MPs were unreliable. Among them were Roman Catholics, nonconformists, Jews and Evangelicals. Somehow the voice of the devout (not to say the high-church) Anglican laity must be made available to them. The Convocations of Canterbury and York had lately met again for the first time since they were closed down during the Bangorian controversy in the early eighteenth century; but they were clerical assemblies, and laymen were not admitted. A

new idea arose: a Church Congress – no more than a peripatetic
annual talking-shop, but with laymen allowed in (and women,
though they would not speak). Medd was now bursar of his
college, and some of the earliest discussions to this end were
held in his rooms. Wilberforce backed the project. The first
Congress was held at Oxford in 1862. Evangelicals stayed away
from it as being an opposition venture; but gradually they
joined in, and Church Congresses had a certain usefulness
until the two Convocations began to accept lay members in the
late 1880s. And at the end of the 1860s Medd took a leading
part in setting up Keble College. It was to serve as a memorial
to Tractarianism's first prophet; and it was designed by William
Butterfield, the movement's leading architect, groping back
into the middle ages in architecture as men like Medd were in
liturgy. Its polychromatic brick intricacies began to go up
opposite the Parks in north Oxford in the year after John
Keble's death.

In October 1870, when he was forty-one, Medd accepted
Liddon's nomination to the rectory of Barnes. The rhythm of
college life demanded it: Medd had for eight years been dean
of the college, living in the first-floor rooms overlooking the
High Street where Stanley had once lived; and it was time to
give place to a younger man. But in December the master of the
college, one Frederick Plumptre, suddenly died. The lure of the
master's lodgings was another thing altogether. Medd let himself be a candidate. 'Some feared', says a subsequent local-paper
obituary notice which shows clear inside knowledge, 'that Medd
was too much wedded to the old traditions, while others, whose
votes determined the matter, had no sympathy with his or any
ecclesiastical tendencies.' (And this at the college which had
sent Shelley down for atheism.) The Life's Record rounds off
the story. 'Escaped being elected master of University by the
turn of one vote, giving seven as against five in favour of
Mr G. G. Bradley, headmaster of Marlborough. *Deo gratias*.'
(Bradley was a liberal in Church affairs who later followed
Stanley at Westminster.)

Medd's vote of thanks to God is underlined twice. Three days
later he was instituted by the bishop of London at Barnes.

He kept his Oxford fellowship; and within a year he had collected a further dignity. He became examining chaplain (scrutineer of aspiring priests) to Bishop Thomas Claughton of Rochester, high-churchman and friend of Wilberforce's. The Tractarians, like the Evangelicals, cherished their own.

His new parishioners will have found his jerky prose hard to listen to after Melvill's silvery cadences. 'And so we,' Medd said to them once in a fair specimen of his pulpit art, 'in this quiet parish, lying, as it does, in many respects, so happily, behind its natural watery entrenchment, which has so far kept at bay the invasion of the great metropolis, even we, whose very neighbourhood to the greatest city in the world makes us prize our own retirement all the more, cannot shut ourselves off as a parish from the general life of the Church and of the nation, in which, as members of the body, we are so deeply interested, and by the movements of which we must ourselves be so nearly affected.'

(The punctuation is from the manuscript he preached from. He would mark syllables he wished to stress with a grave accent in red crayon.)

In fact Medd saw to it that Barnes, so far from being shut off from the life of the Church, was drawn sharply into its controversies. He put candles on the altar. There were two on the embroidered, lace-fringed cloth with which he covered the table itself, and four more higher up and to the sides. It was a sight not seen in that church before. The significance of a gorgeous altar, to the high-church mind, was that at a communion service it showed Christ's body and blood to be really present under the form of bread and wine: in other words, the service became not a mere commemoration but a renewed sacrifice – an interpretation both allowed and disallowed within the Book of Common Prayer.

It was a new interest for high-churchmen. The first Tractarians had been concerned purely for the renewal of doctrine: Pusey was against any obstruction of that effort by provocative trappings. But by the 1870s the high-church emphasis was on the reform of ritual. Symbols mattered: they drew their importance from what Medd called 'that sacramental system whereby an inward gift of grace is connected with an outward and visible sign, which is one of the special features of His Church as a divine and supernatural institution'. (It was the same principle which Melvill had dismissed as 'the substitution of means for an end'.) Late in life Medd came round, in retrospect, to the Pusey view; but at the time he entered zestfully into the fray. When he arrived at Barnes, a Brighton vicar named John Purchas was already being taken through the Church courts for (among other things) using altar candles and incense. The Privy Council found Purchas in breach of the law. Medd signed a remonstrance to the archbishops and bishops. By 1874 low-church agitation against the ritualists obliged Disraeli to push a Public Worship Regulation Bill through Parliament (which he did with the more willingness because Gladstone was a high-churchman). Medd put his name to what he called 'a largely signed declaration against the enforcement of "a rigid uniformity in divine worship" '. The Bill passed into law, but fell swiftly into discredit and disuse. Medd himself was never troubled by it.

His stance is sufficiently made clear in his single volume of sermons, called *Sermons preached in the Parish Church of Barnes, 1871 to 1876.* (The title is truthful as far as it goes, but it does not exclude the same sermons' having been preached in other places as well. His manuscript of one of them, on conscious religion – 'We must order our lives as in his sight; we must consciously make God's will our rule' – has in neat boxes round the heading and text the following entries: 'preached in College, Feb. 5, 1865; Parish Ch., Banbury, Dec. 1866; St John Bapt. Oxon., March 24, 1867; Newland, Sept. 8, 1867; Coll. chapel, May 3, 1868;· St Mary's, Oxford, Aug. 30, 1868; do. Cambridge, March 12, 1869; Barnes, morn. of Jun. 15, 1871; St Matthew's, City Road, dedication week, Sund. Sept. 24, 1871; Watermoor, 5 Nov. 1876, evening.' That was ten outings for the piece in twelve years, to learned congregations and simple.) He protested for form's sake against categorization: could anyone, he asked, who had thoroughly imbibed Christian ideas, 'suffer himself without protest to be ticketed with this or that exclusive epithet as *high*, or *low*, or *broad*?' But the label he himself

preferred was 'Catholic', a term which has never quite returned
to its non-partisan, Prayer-Book sense. His attitudes were of a
piece: his congregation will have found them in bewildering
contrast to Melvill's.

In common with many Tractarians, some of whom did heroic
work in the East End of London, Medd was more inclined than
Melvill had been to urge 'bodily works of mercy'. If Jesus had
fixed any fare to heaven, it was these, rather than personal
conversion. 'He tells us', declared Medd, 'that the test by which
he will separate the sheep and the goats is their attention to, or
their neglect of, the duty of ministering to the natural wants and
bodily sufferings of their fellow-creatures'.

But in fact salvation was 'a gift, purely a gift of God, just as
life is'. All that needed to be said was that the gift ought to have
certain consequences. 'The salvation which Christ long since
secured for us all has already been made over to us individually,
as a covenant possession, at our baptism. What we have to do is
to use and to cherish the gift – to guard against the loss or
forfeiture of it.' The way to do that was through the services of
the Church, and in particular the eucharist: 'the flesh and
blood of Christ – as the second Adam, the life-giving Spirit – is
the antidote and cure of the evil and corruption that is in us'.
For that reason Christ was 'the one and only mediator through
whom our true life can be restored to us'. That nevertheless left
to Medd as priest the function of 'the leader and the mouth-
piece of your solemn, yet most joyous, eucharistic worship'. He
called it 'my high and sacred duty'. He was a confessed
sacerdotalist, a believer in the special power of the priesthood.
In a learned article at this same period he argued against 'the
use of the word "sacerdotalism" as a term of reproach and
contempt'.

A notable absentee from Medd's sermons, as compared with
Melvill's, was the Old Testament. He barely mentioned it. As
for the conflict between geology and Genesis which had begun
to trouble churchmen fifty years before, Medd cunningly
deferred the problem. Christianity had nothing to fear from
fuller enquiry: our difficulty was only that enquiry had not yet
gone far enough. 'Much of imagined opposition between

scientific truth and revealed truth is simply apparent, not real;
the temporary result of imperfect knowledge of one or the other,
or of both.' Churchmen had begun to bury the problem in
bland neglect.

Medd was still a bachelor. His mother's younger sister kept
house for him. The sermons are dedicated 'to my aunt, Emily
Goldsmith, to whose loving criticism these sermons, and to
whose manifold help, not I only, but the parish of Barnes, are
greatly indebted'. But there was a younger woman who lived in
another big house, Byfeld House, on the further side of the
church. Louisa Nesbitt, twenty years younger than Medd, was
the eldest child of a City hide-merchant. She used later to tell
her children that she had been cross at being called from some
pleasure to entertain the new rector. But in the course of five
years her feelings softened. She may even have trembled a little
when she heard him rolling off texts from the pulpit about how
'In the resurrection they neither marry nor are given in
marriage', or how 'They that are Christ's have crucified the
flesh with its passions and lusts': Tractarians had an equivocal
attitude to marriage, and many chose celibacy. Not Medd. He
and his Louie were married in his church in January 1876. The
final spur was Medd's impending departure: towards the end of
1875 he was offered, and accepted, the cure of souls of a small
Gloucestershire village – North Cerney, near Cirencester. The
Medds moved in March.

The move was sufficiently explained by the fact that North
Cerney was one of the best livings in the gift of Medd's college.
His predecessor, also a fellow of University, had spent the last
forty-eight years of his life there; Medd spent the last thirty-three.
One can see why. It was an ideal country-parson's posting at the
very end of the period when the lot of the country parson could
still be enviable: a page from Trollope, even Jane Austen; in a
double sense a pastoral idyll. At Barnes, with 4,400 people in the
parish, Medd's annual income had been £415. At North Cerney
he had 687 parishioners (their leading figure Lord Bathurst),
and his income was £920. He gave up his fellowship, after one
more year; but he had collected its final benefit, and could live
in gentlemanly state, riding round his domain in the valley of

Peter and Louisa Medd at North Cerney

the river Churn and on the downs beside. The honey-coloured
Queen Anne rectory, even handsomer than the house Hare had
built at Barnes, had three acres of grounds: beyond the lawns
and the shrubbery and the great three-trunked beech (known of
course as the Trinity beech) there was a huge kitchen garden,
and pasturage where the Medds kept three cows as well as a
horse.

That same year Medd was offered the bishopric of Brechin,
in the uninviting north-east of Scotland. He turned it down: the
decision can have cost him little effort. He was already, at
forty-seven, taking happily to a settled life and fatherhood. His
first son was born on the last day of that year: five more
followed – the last of them born when Medd was sixty-three –
and two daughters.

But he did more than enjoy the comforts of rural life and the
married state. He restored his enchanting little late-medieval
church and rebuilt its chancel: Tractarians were great beauti-
fiers of chancels, in their effort to reverse the trend of eighteenth-
century and Evangelical devotion and bring the worshipper's
chief attention back from the pulpit to the altar. He introduced
daily matins and a new hymn-book – *Hymns Ancient and Modern*.
He examined theological students for Oxford and ordination
candidates for his friend Bishop Claughton (now of St Albans:
he had chosen that half of his enormous old diocese when it was
divided, and he made Medd an honorary canon there). He
preached at St Paul's. He became a governor of Cheltenham
Ladies' College, a dozen miles to the north, on the nomination
of his university. And he wrote the 1882 Bampton Lectures – the
annual series of eight divinity lectures at Oxford set up under
the will of a Canon John Bampton of Salisbury.

Medd called them, and the resulting book, *The One Mediator*.
His central point was that Christ's mediating office between
God and his world had existed since the beginning of creation.
His Oxford obituarist, writing both in *The Times* and in the
Gloucestershire papers, found the lectures 'distinguished by
great learning and an unusual wealth of illustration, but their
style and condensed character prevented them from ever
becoming popular'. The twentieth-century reader readily sees

the point. They contain a good many passages Germanic in their inspissated mysticism and their prodigality of capital letters: 'In a past Eternity, before Time was, God, Father, Son and Holy Spirit rested in the Manifestation of Himself to Himself, blest in the overflowing Love of the Divine Persons each to other; yet contemplating all possible action, Creation included (since Creation did take place) as presently realized to him in whose Absolute and Infinite and purely Spiritual Existence there is no Past, Present, or Future.'

Despite their resoundingly Protestant title, the lectures put forward an uncompromisingly high doctrine of the priesthood. Of Jesus's apostles at the Last Supper Medd declared: 'He had chosen them to be the seed and beginning of that subordinate representative priesthood in his Kingdom, whereby, in visible earthly form necessitated by the cessation of His natural Presence, His supreme sole Priesthood as the Only Mediator should, through all generations of the Church below, until He should come again, be, instrumentally but effectually, exercised and exhibited.' Jesus was the one mediator; but in his absence, priests ordained in the apostolic succession were his sole agents. It was a doctrine which claimed peculiar authority for the Anglican and Roman Catholic clergy, and read nonconformist ministers out of their functions altogether.

Low-church Anglicans came off hardly better. Medd spoke tartly of 'the narrowness of view which thinks only of future individual salvation, and is a ready prey to that spirit of disunion and separation which is the bane of modern Christianity'. But there was a graceful touch at the end. In one of the notes at the back of the book, seeking support for his reading of a knotty point in Hebrews, Medd turned – clearly to his own surprise – to Melvill. 'Let me here earnestly commend the attention of my readers', he wrote, 'to the valuable and interesting exposition by my venerated predecessor in the parish of Barnes, the late Canon Melvill'. And he proceeded to a five-page quotation from a Melvill sermon of fifty years before. (It was the one which exalted the minister's function as God's messenger; but Melvill had been thinking there chiefly of the ministry of the word, not the sacrament.) Medd had a name for forbearance in party strife, and he here displayed it. But his moderation was no more than moderate. He could not forbear adding *O si sic omnes*! If only they were all like that!

Medd's Bamptons revived his academic standing, and his own affection for academic life after more than a dozen years of choir festivals and flower shows, to the point where in 1885 he let his name go forward for two Oxford professorships; but he got neither. He settled back into his given level of existence. His friends and relations came to stay, and he went to stay with them – with Bright, now a canon at Christ Church, with King in the Old Palace at Lincoln. He gave a parish jubilee dinner, in the flaming June which marked Queen Victoria's fifty years on the throne, under the rectory's avenue of elms. He spent a summer holiday as chaplain to the English community at Engelberg in the Swiss Alps. He was a pallbearer at Claughton's funeral at St Albans. He indulged his Toryism: he chafed over 'Mr Gladstone's idiotic Home Rule, Ireland, Bill', and rejoiced at the downfall of the Rosebery ministry – 'the most mischievous, unprincipled and discreditable that England has seen in my lifetime'. He took his children to their boarding-schools, or to Eights Week at Oxford. He gave his friends medical advice by letter, remembering what he had picked up from his surgeon father. He and Louie ('my heart's darling, my helpmeet, my deaconess') were invited to a surprise party at the village school and presented with a salver, a bouquet and a glass vase in honour of their twenty-five years in the village and the married state. Medd was nearly seventy-one: the numbered pages in the Life's Record had given out at seventy, the scriptural allowance, and he was into the blank pages at the back.

He suffered from gout; and infirmity confined him more and more to his study. He was much consulted, by letter, about the writing of prayers and the ordering of services. He had done one last learned work: an edition of a seventeenth-century gathering of Greek and Latin devotions. They came to him from Oxford on tiny gilt-edged pages, the vellum binding held together with green silk ribbon; and they were a memento of two Caroline divines to whom the Tractarians had especially looked. They had been compiled by Andrewes and given by him, a little before his death, to Laud.

Medd himself died in 1908, at the age of seventy-nine. He had preached in North Cerney church less than three weeks before, from a wheel-chair. He was buried under a yew-tree just outside the window of his reconstructed chancel. Over his grave the choir sang a single verse of a hymn by the greatest of Victorian translators from the Latin (and Greek), the Tractarian John Mason Neale: 'Jerusalem the golden'. The chosen verse was the last:

> O sweet and blessed country,
> The home of God's elect!
> O sweet and blessed country
> That eager hearts expect . . .

And among the pile of wreaths left behind when the singers departed was one with an inscription which, as livings like North Cerney dwindled, would not often be seen again. It read: 'With deep sympathy, from the maids at the rectory'.

8 'Sing alleluia forth' (1845-1893)

THE HYMN SUNG OVER MEDD'S GRAVE REPRESENTED A revolution. At the beginning of the nineteenth century most Anglicans sang no hymns at all, unless you count banal metricated versions of the Psalms. By the end of the century they were singing thousands: a few disinterred from Latin and Greek, many borrowed from the great eighteenth-century free-churchmen, most freshly written in Anglican parsonages. A man who bore a leading part in that remarkable development was Medd's successor at Barnes, John Ellerton.

Ellerton wrote about eighty hymns, the best known of them 'The day thou gavest, Lord, is ended'. (It was a Sunday evening hymn, roared out with peculiar fervour in countless school chapels as the shadows closed over another unregretted boarding-school Sunday. In the 1950s and 1960s it took on a new resonance as an elegy on the passing of British power overseas. Although the hymn was ostensibly about the mission field, the couplet 'The sun that bids us rest is waking Our brethren 'neath the western sky' drew an unmistakable parallel between the Church of God and the British empire, notoriously the place the sun never set on; and then the last verse, as if sensing a lift of the divine eyebrow, began, 'So be it, Lord; thy throne shall never, Like earth's proud empires, pass away . . .') Ellerton also stands in the third main nineteenth-century Anglican tradition – after the low and the high, the broad; and his early sympathies lay with a movement much developed by broad-churchmen, Christian Socialism.

He took on that tinge at Cambridge. He came of educated and mildly Evangelical parents – his mother wrote children's

stories with titles like 'How little Fanny learned to be useful' –
and spent a quiet boyhood in London and at Ulverston in north
Lancashire. (He reminisced at the end of his life about 'the old
Lancashire garden, with its thrushes and its damask roses, and
the limestone hills, and the Sunday bells from the grey tower'.)
Then after going away to school on the Isle of Man, and reading
for a year with an Evangelical vicar in the Lake District, he
went up to Trinity, Cambridge, in 1845. There he moved in a
freer intellectual atmosphere than had greeted the young
Melvill: his best friend was F. J. A. Hort, later one of the great
names in the scientific – as distinct from the purely reverential –
examination of the New Testament text. In these surroundings
he found himself reading the work of Frederick Denison
Maurice, an agonized seeker after Christian truth who taught
at King's College, London.

Ellerton found Maurice's big book *The Kingdom of Christ* heavy
going, but he 'fagged on' at it. In the very early days of trade
unions, the book foresaw a world without class distinctions and
without oppression. It became the handbook of the Christian
Socialists. Maurice had also made friends with another clerical
radical, Charles Kingsley. 'The wise and brave Charles
Kingsley', Ellerton called him; and when Kingsley began to
publish novels – *Yeast*, *Alton Locke*, tract-like and yet powerful
pieces about the miseries of working-class life – they became
lifelong favourites on Ellerton's shelves.

Besides that, Maurice encouraged a non-partisan approach
to Christian doctrine. He professed himself against broad-
churchmanship, on the ground that it settled doctrinal disputes
merely by abandoning disputed doctrines; but he encouraged
free-ranging doubts indistinguishable from it. 'After three or
four of his books', Ellerton wrote later, 'you will be accustomed
to his peculiarities, the strange *flashes* of deep insight, the
reverent hesitation and fear of mis-statements which makes
people call him hazy; and his worst fault in the eyes of the
common herd of readers is, that he refuses to tell you what your
opinion is to be, but will have you think about a question, and
generally leaves you with the impression that you have been
talking nonsense very positively in all you have hitherto said

about it.' In 1853 Maurice was found not to believe in everlasting punishment – a difficult deduction from his cloudy
prose – and was dismissed from his two professorships at King's.
The sacking only increased his influence.

Ellerton also admired the writing of Arthur Hugh Clough,
who early used the label broad-church, and of Tennyson, a
friend of Maurice's. *In Memoriam*, published in 1850 and
stretching out 'lame hands of faith', anxious to believe and yet
painfully aware of the difficulties, was a broad-church poem.
Broad-churchmanship was the continuation in Anglicanism of
the spirit of free and rational enquiry.

The sympathies conceived at Cambridge remained with
Ellerton all his life. Ordained a year after he went down, he
served his first curacy at Easebourne, outside Midhurst, in
Sussex, where he and his now widowed mother spent three
placid years within sight of the ancient oaks of Cowdray Park.
The local archdeacon was a former Trinity don, Julius Hare, a
great-grandson of Francis Hare: he and Maurice married each
other's sisters, and Hare roused the same kind of wrath as
Maurice for tolerating informed doubt. It was probably Hare
who brought Ellerton to Easebourne; and Hare certainly
helped him onward to a senior curacy at Brighton parish church.
In 1860 Ellerton was promoted to be vicar of Crewe Green, a
village on the edge of Crewe. (He took a newly-acquired wife
with him, and his mother too, for the first six years of marriage.)
There the duty of answering a visiting free-thinker drew from
him a courteous and complete enunciation of broad-church
principles. 'Most cordially', it said in part, 'do I join Mr G——
in proclaiming the "*right* of every man to think for himself";
only I would rather call it the *duty*. God forbid that I should
dictate to any man what he is to believe, if that dictating
implies that he is to believe it because I tell him so. The first
Christian teachers declared that by manifestation of the truth
they commended themselves to every man's conscience. I desire
no more. But if it be truth indeed that a man receives in his
conscience, that truth will make him free.'

The patron of Crewe Green was a devout peer named Lord
Crewe. Sir George Gilbert Scott (later the architect of the

Albert Memorial and St Pancras Station in London) had just
built him a new brick church. As Lord Crewe's domestic
chaplain, Ellerton said prayers daily at Crewe Hall; the
seventeenth-century chapel there was reopened (with the help of
the archbishop of York, the bishop of Chester, and most of the
clergy and choir of Chester Cathedral) during Ellerton's time.
But Ellerton was not tempted away from the chance to put the
principles of Maurice and Kingsley into practice. Crewe was
already a railway town; and Ellerton began to be busy at the
Mechanics' Institution which the London & North-Western
Railway Company ran there for its workforce. He reorganized
the library and the evening classes, and taught English history
and Old Testament history himself. A manager at the railway
works remembered his faithfulness: 'The unwearied patience
with which night after night he would trudge into dirty, black,
smoky Crewe, bringing with him an air of wide-reaching
interests and warm sympathy for the toiling masses, made a
deep impression; and he gradually won his way into the hearts
of large numbers of the artisans, to whom such a character was
somewhat novel. The writer has frequently heard expressions of
wonder from onlookers, themselves artisans – "what it could be
that led Mr Ellerton to take so much trouble to teach the lads
from whom he had nothing to expect in return, and who were
not worth the expenditure of time so valuable in other directions as his was known to be". Among those mechanics who
were themselves inspired by the same zeal, this self-devotion
caused him to be greatly loved and honoured with a love and
honour which deepened and extended as the years went on.
There were but few capable of appropriating the ideas he set
before them on history, poetry or scripture exegesis, but all
could see that he was working without thought of reward, and
many were fascinated by the beauty of such an example of
self-devotion.' On the Institution's council, moreover, he was a
pre-eminent peacemaker, because 'he possessed the faculty of
never perceiving a rudeness directed against himself'.

Ellerton himself was in no doubt why he did it. He believed,
and acted on the belief, that one life and one sphere of service
was as precious to God as another. He said on the Sunday after

a young railwayman's funeral: 'We honour the soldier who gives his life upon the field, in obedience to the call of duty; or the sailor who goes down in his sinking ship in giving or in carrying out his orders. And surely it is just as heroic, just as honourable, to be found faithful to death in any other service to which a man has been called; to care more for doing our daily work well, than for doing it easily; to treat it not merely as a means of getting bread, but as a task which it is a duty to God to do thoroughly, and a sin against God to do carelessly.'

At the funeral, one of Ellerton's own hymns was sung. It was during his twelve years at Crewe Green that he put together his national reputation as a hymn-writer and hymnologist. For him it was no new activity. At Cambridge he had founded with Hort a college literary group called the Attic Society to which he read his own verses – 'rendered still more striking', another friend recalled, 'by the fine, deep, emotional tone in which he read them to us'. At Brighton he began writing hymns. The first of them were for children – 'The hours of school are over', and so on; and he put four of his own efforts, and four translations by Hort, into a slim volume published in 1859 under the title *Hymns for Schools and Bible Classes*.

It was a time when writing and compiling hymns was a widespread pursuit. Since 1820, new hymn-books had been coming off the presses at the rate of about two a year. Anglicans were joyfully rediscovering a very old form of worship. It was a wholly natural form: it was such an expression of corporate happiness, such a potential delight to heart and ear, that Christians had always supposed it a principal activity among angels. Yet Anglicans had barely been practising it at all. The nearest they had come had been to sing a New Version, or tortured verse paraphrase, of the Psalms: that had been the only activity with sufficient scriptural basis to win approval from the dominant thinkers of the English Reformation. But during the eighteenth century certain nonconformist hymn-writers, notably Isaac Watts and John Wesley's brother Charles, began to show that non-scriptural words too could be illuminating and uplifting; and towards the end of that century Evangelicals within the Church of England began first borrow-

ing these hymns and then imitating them. It is one of the great
gifts which the dissenting tradition has conferred on the
Anglican. That whole period was not a particularly favourable
one for English poetry, and many of the new hymns were
uncomfortably close to doggerel; but the standard of writing
was much improved as the Tractarians – a highly educated
group, and concerned to demonstrate Anglicanism's continuity
with the pre-Reformation Church – joined the movement with
translations from Greek, medieval Latin, and German. 'There
is scarcely any event in the history of our church worship during
the past sixty years so great and so remarkable as the substitution
of hymns for metrical psalms', Ellerton was able to write in the
Churchman's Family Magazine in 1864. 'It came to us from an
unwelcome source – from the dissenters, eminently from the
Methodists; it was first adopted by those of the clergy who
sympathized most with them; for many long years it was that
dreaded thing, a "party badge"; but it held its ground until
wise men of all parties began to recognize its value. First as
supplementary to the New Version, and then as replacing it,
hymns found their way into hitherto inaccessible quarters; and
the revolution is at last complete.'

At Crewe Green, as at all his churches, Ellerton was at pains
to see that his congregation made the most of this new opportunity. 'Now a congregation', he wrote for the same magazine,
'consists of four divisions: first, those who *can* and *do* sing;
secondly, those who *can* and *don't*; thirdly, those who *can't* and
do; and fourthly, those who *can't* and *don't*. All four of these
divisions must be affected by the singing. The first, whether
nominally members of the choir or no, are the natural leaders
of the service of song, and through them you must influence the
rest; the second must be encouraged and cultivated till they
pass into the first; the third must be kindly borne with and
tolerated, till they are drowned by the first two; while the last
will assuredly feel and enjoy the power of true congregational
worship; they too will make melody with their hearts, though
God has seen fit to deny them the privilege of doing so with
their lips.'

But he did more than encourage or tolerate his Crewe Green

flock. He gave it something to sing. In such time as he could
save from the baronial chapel, the Gilbert Scott church and the
Mechanics' Institution he wrote most of the hymns for which he
became well known. 'Sing alleluia forth in duteous praise' was
the first of them, a translation from a Latin original used in the
early Christian centuries in Spain. Another translation was
'Welcome happy morning! age to age shall say', a version of the
'*Salve festa dies*' of Venantius Fortunatus, bishop of Poitiers at the
end of the sixth century. A third was 'O strength and stay
upholding all creation', from an evening hymn in Latin
attributed to St Ambrose, fourth-century bishop of Milan. It
made use of the familiar parallel, which Ellerton particularly
liked, between the close of day and the close of life:

> Grant to life's day a calm unclouded ending,
> An eve untouched by shadows of decay,
> The brightness of a holy death-bed blending
> With dawning glories of the eternal day.

The rest of this group were originals. There was another
evening hymn, written for a festival at Nantwich, and specifically
meant as the last hymn on a Sunday evening; 'Saviour, again
to thy dear name we raise With one accord our parting hymn of
praise'. It asked in successive verses for the grant of peace 'upon
our homeward way', 'through the coming night', and 'throughout our earthly life'. There was a Sunday morning hymn, 'This
is the day of light'. There was a hymn for weekday lunch-time
services, 'Behold us, Lord, a little space': Ellerton liked hymns
to fit the occasion, and he owed part of his fame to the fact that
this made them easy for clergymen to choose. There was a hymn
about the conversion of St Paul, 'We sing the glorious conquest'.
There was a funeral hymn, 'Now the labourer's task is o'er',
with its refrain:

> Father, in thy gracious keeping
> Leave we now thy servant sleeping,

and its tune by the Tractarian musician J. B. Dykes, which for
at least half a century was almost as familiar an accompaniment
of Anglican burials as the ninetieth Psalm.

And there was 'The day thou gavest, Lord, is ended'. It became Ellerton's most famous line. By one of the ironies of fame, it was a line he did not write himself. He borrowed it from a hymn in an 1855 collection called *Church Poetry*; and there no author's name is given. But the ingenious new theme, that the sun may go down on the day but not on the Church, is Ellerton's own.

Besides writing hymns, he found time to compile hymn-books. By the 1860s the multiplicity of hymn-books was becoming a nuisance. Worshippers in a church which was not their own, even if they came from another church in the same town, would find an unfamiliar book in their hands. With the market so fragmented, no hymn-books could sell in any quantity, and all were expensive. The diversity gave a greater sense of disunity within the Church of England than was in fact true. *Hymns Ancient and Modern* was the first hymn-book designed to meet these problems by achieving a wide sale: it was put together by a team of clerics under Sir Henry Baker, baronet incumbent of the Herefordshire hamlet of Monkland. But when it was first published in 1861 it was not a big book, and over-indulgent to the high-church side at that. (It contained a piece of straightforward mariolatry by Sir Henry himself, beginning 'Shall we not love thee, Mother dear?') The Society for Promoting Christian Knowledge decided to make its own attempt at producing a hymn-book which could go into general Anglican use. Ellerton was early consulted, and became one of the three editors. Another was a Shropshire rector, William Walsham How (who wrote 'For all the saints'). The first musical editor was Arthur Sullivan. The result, *Church Hymns*, was published in 1871. Thirty-nine of the hymns in it were by Ellerton. He was already at work on a commentary to all six hundred hymns in the book, giving details of their author and their textual history.

Writing, compiling and annotating hymns was becoming his main work. He was exactly the kind of man who ought to have become a cathedral canon, where he would have had time for research, varied services to find hymns for, and a good choir to sing them. But he still lived in the era – though near the end of it – when the natural haven for church scholarship was the country parsonage. In 1872 he moved a little south from Crewe to the Shropshire village of Hinstock, where a newish red-brick rectory surveyed a newish red-sandstone church standing on a mound in the middle of a main road. Here he had both more leisure and more money than at Crewe. He wrote a few more hymns of his own – notably 'Throned upon the awful tree' (a meditation on the cry of dereliction from the Cross), and a wedding hymn commissioned by the duke of Westminster for his daughter. Chiefly, though, he put together a children's hymn-book with Walsham How, whose rectory at Whittington was on the other side of the county, towards Wales; and he went on with his commentary on *Church Hymns*, making laborious train-journeys to Cambridge when he needed to look things up in libraries.

He was backing the wrong book. *Hymns Ancient and Modern* was steadily overtaking it. An appendix had already been added to *Ancient and Modern*, and in 1875 a revised edition was brought out which steadily established it as the most useful, because by now the most comprehensive, Anglican collection. Ellerton went on with his long work; but by the time his commentary was published, as an introduction to a huge and unusable folio edition of *Church Hymns* in 1881, that book was doomed to pass out of use. His learning was not wasted: the 1889 *Ancient and Modern* had him as an active helper.

Ellerton's value to the history of Anglican hymn-singing was that he possessed an educated judgment and set it to work. In the years when a canon of hymns was being established which was to last for the best part of a century, Ellerton did as much as anyone to guide taste, both by choosing hymns and by writing them. He perfectly understood that the hymn was only marginally an art form. Its function was too defined. It was an expression of the feelings of worship. 'Here we must fix our limit', he said. 'Hymns may express adoration, thanksgiving, commemoration of God's mercies: they may be prayers, penitential, supplicatory, intercessory; they may be devout aspirations after God; but in any case they must be forms of worship.' That ruled out a great deal of the descriptive or introspective material which might have been the stuff of poetry. 'We cannot always expect real poetry', Ellerton went on, 'even in a good hymn.' What we could expect was that hymns should be sincere (being what they professed to be, a form of worship, and therefore eschewing covert controversial allusions or 'theatrical displays of emotion'); vigorous, with 'power to embody in themselves the characteristics of the time which gave them birth'; simple – not vulgar or puerile, but in plain language; brief – not more than eight four-line stanzas; and adapted to music, without complex or greatly varied metres.

In applying these principles, he could sometimes be severe. He spoke of 'the sensuousness, the effeminacy, or the empty jingle of such hymns as "Oh come and mourn with me awhile", "Jesu meek and lowly", or "Nearer, my God, to thee" '. He disapproved, when he considered the Neale translation ('Jerusalem the golden') sung over Medd's grave, of 'its plaintiveness, its softness and its lusciousness'. He found the hymns of F. W. Faber hysterical and painful. But those were stylistic judgments. He was not objecting to the fact that Neale was a Tractarian, or Faber a convert to Rome. Ellerton had a proper broad-churchman's perception that a hymn-book would only deserve general use if it comprehended high as well as low. 'It is easy to try to steer a safe course by omitting what will offend one or other school in the Church', he wrote to a fellow editor for the SPCK; 'but often the result is to leave a mere dull residuum of that which is certainly common to both, but which satisfies the faith of neither. Surely if each side (within due limits) were *represented* in a hymnal, as it is in our Prayer Book, the object of wide and common use would be attained in a nobler and more effectual way'.

As a writer of hymns, he conformed pretty well to his own demands as a compiler. He was certainly a model author in point of character. Not merely did he always waive copyright or any fee, choosing to regard his hymns as 'a gift to the Church of Christ', when other people asked to reprint or use them; he also – even more strikingly in a writer – tolerated having them altered. 'Hard things are often said by living writers as to the mutilation of their hymns by compilers', he acknowledged to a

Church Congress at Stoke during his time nearby at Hinstock.
'May it be permitted for one whose own hymns have not
escaped this unpleasant process to say a word on the other side?
– that anyone who presumes to lay his offering of a song of
praise upon the altar, not for his own, but for God's glory,
cannot be too thankful for the devout, thoughtful and scholarly
criticism of those whose object it is to make his work less
unworthy of its sacred purpose.'

More importantly, he kept his own rules of style. He
addressed God; he used sentiments which are at once recog-
nizable as the accents of his own time; he did it plainly,
tersely and tidily, so that the result could be sung. Consider:

> Grant us thy peace upon our homeward way;
> With thee began, with thee shall end, the day:
> Guard thou the lips from sin, the hearts from shame,
> That in this house have called upon thy name.

It had the further merit, a considerable one in England, that
although openly moralistic it stopped short of being embarras-
sing: people could use these words in each other's hearing and
not blush. It was, in a word, congregational.

Ellerton's hymns could in consequence be judged 'bearable
to the cultured, and instructive to the devout': it was the cool
verdict of Julian's *Dictionary of Hymnology*. John Julian, another
scholar of the parsonage, walled in to his Yorkshire vicarage
with innumerable hymn-books, knew a great deal more about
hymns than Ellerton did; but he hardly ever put his neck on the
block to the extent of writing any. Ellerton traded devotedly
with such talents as he had. Throughout his own lifetime his
stock rose steadily: he had no hymns in the 1861 edition of
Ancient and Modern, three in the 1868, ten in the 1875, and
twenty-six in the 1889. Even in the current edition, which dates
from 1922, Ellerton has eleven original hymns and four
translations. That figure for original hymns is exceeded only by
Charles Wesley with thirty, Watts with seventeen and Mrs
Alexander with thirteen. (The runaway winner on translations
is Neale, with forty-six.) In the next major recension the Ellertons will dwindle: the congregations are no longer there to sing

all those Sunday evening hymns. But Ellerton, unassuming soul, would have been astonished to have held on so long. He would have expected the period of innovation which he represented to be itself sooner renewed.

It was from Hinstock that Ellerton moved to Barnes. The opportunity came after only four years, in 1876, because of Medd's move to North Cerney. In a busy parish, Ellerton's work on hymns had perforce to continue in a lower key. He finally brought out his massive commentary. He helped compile a fresh *Children's Hymn-Book*, supplied with hymns which were judged to be within the spiritual experience of the average confirmation candidate. ('To me it is simple *misery*', he wrote to the editor, Mrs Carey Brock, 'to hear a noisy Sunday school singing "Abide with me".') He put together a *London Mission Hymn-Book*. He wrote a number of special hymns: for a new daughter-church at Barnes; for a children's flower service at Chelsea, where an old Trinity friend was rector; for the opening of a 'coffee tavern', where workmen might be served something other than alcohol. But 'he was priest first, and only after that a poet', his curate at Barnes, Henry Housman, wrote in a memoir of him; and at Barnes he found a good deal for a priest to do.

The canon of St Paul's who appointed him was Joseph Lightfoot, who at the same time held a chair of divinity at Cambridge. Lightfoot had been another near-contemporary at Trinity, along with Hort and B. F. Westcott. Lightfoot and Westcott were Hort's companion stars in the firmament of Cambridge New Testament scholarship; and they went on to become, one after the other, notably sympathetic bishops of the largely industrial diocese of Durham. Ellerton was thus returning to his Cambridge background – the company of men who could reconcile independent thought and a Christian concern for the poor.

The poor were by now a noticeable presence even in the outer suburbs of London. Cramped streets of terraced cottages were being laid out for them at a great rate in the fields on the western edge of Barnes, beyond the embanked railway-line which crossed the Thames at Barnes Bridge. In 1878 Ellerton

John Ellerton

sent a letter about the problems to his diocesan, Bishop Thorold of Rochester. (Barnes was much subject to changes of diocese in the reorganizations of these years, passing from Winchester through London and Rochester into the new diocese of Southwark in 1905.) 'This isolated district of Westfields', Ellerton wrote, 'is *the* problem we have to solve in our church work in Barnes. It is cut off by a railway embankment from the parish church, so that there is no carriage-road to it, except from the Mortlake side, and only winding, dark and dirty footpaths; yet there are 1,200 people, all, except a few clerks, etc., of the working class.'

The flight from the inner city had begun. But therein lay the temporary solution: left behind were redundant places of worship. There was one in Red Lion Square, in Holborn. 'I should have deferred all these details till I had the pleasure of welcoming your Lordship at our confirmation,' Ellerton went on, 'but that within the last few days we have had an offer of an exceedingly convenient temporary church, built of iron externally, wood-lined, with a good slate roof, and all fittings complete, for £80. This will hold two hundred people. It has been surveyed for us by two professional friends, an architect and a civil engineer, who both strongly recommend its purchase.'

Bishop Thorold gave his assent, and the corrugated-iron tabernacle was duly translated from Red Lion Square to Westfields. Housman was put in charge of it, till he went off to teach Hebrew at the newish theological college at Chichester; his successor as Ellerton's curate was Russell Wakefield, later a bishop of Birmingham. The Westfields mission, like so many in the poor districts of big cities, was a focus for the high-minded devotion of a whole string of burly, cassocked curates. After six years Ellerton was able to write in his sporadically-appearing parish magazine: 'There are many churches in the neighbourhood with elaborate music, and large, wealthy congregations; there are few, if any, in the neighbourhood which, in the simple heartiness and unaffected reverence with which divine service is rendered, are more touching than this humble little iron shed.'

In the more numinous Gothic spaces of the parish church,

darkened by the enormous yew-tree at the door, Ellerton preached his own accumulated thoughts – and with some care, given a congregation of increasing numbers and education. Although he tolerated the ritual Medd had introduced, he hoped to 'spiritualize' it by giving an equal prominence to the ministry of the word. Like Medd as well as Melvill, he published his Barnes sermons; and the title he gave them, *The Holiest Manhood*, a phrase from the prologue of *In Memoriam*, was an explicit statement of his broad-church lineage.

In the first sermon in the book, 'On the child Jesus in the Temple', he upheld the need for continued free enquiry into Christianity's claims, so long as it was reverently done. He rebuked, by implication, the low-churchmen for barricading themselves behind the Bible and the high-churchmen for ignoring the problem in a cloud of mysticism. 'If now new and wider thoughts about God and his will,' he said, 'about creation, about nature, about the end and the future of man are stirring in the minds of thinking people, we ought not to fear them. Only let us recollect how the wisest and the holiest one asked his questions: it was within his Father's house, it was under the hallowing influence of his worship.'

He dissented from Melvill and the Evangelicals (though never by name) over their silence in the matter of a social gospel. 'The popular notion of salvation', he declared, 'makes it all centre in blessings bestowed upon the individual man. He is called, he is convinced of sin, he is born again, he is forgiven, and so he is saved, and ready to be translated to glory. And then he is to do no more, except thank God forever for saving him. It is a miserable mutilation and perversion of the gospel – the very glorification of selfishness.' For he who called us to salvation, Ellerton pursued, called us to action. 'The servants had money given them to trade with. The virgins had lamps given them to light the dark path of life for those who, like themselves, were followers of the bridegroom. We ought not to think of a life of active Christian charity as the high and rare privilege of a few saintly and elected souls. It is the life set before each, and Christ gives power to each to live it.'

That was the emphasis of Ellerton's whole life: on using the gifts of God as given. In contradistinction to the Tractarians (and to certain later Evangelicals), he was doubtful of the virtue of mere abstinence in any sphere. Though he recognized the problem of self-indulgence, he said: 'I do not desire to exaggerate the evils of our time. In every generation the theme of the preacher has been the luxury, the extravagance, the licence, the irreligion around him. In some respects we are better than our fathers. We have outgrown the unbridled insolence of the middle ages, the shameless coarseness of the eighteenth century.' He addressed himself in particular to the problem of drink, which preoccupied churchmen at the time. Ellerton was well disposed towards the temperance movement; he helped the compilers of a *Temperance Hymn-Book*; but he was not himself a teetotaller, and he knew why. He recalled Jesus's miracle at the Cana wedding. 'In the strongest possible way he sanctioned the use of wine, not for health or medicine, but as a help in social enjoyment. I think that those of us who are setting themselves to take part in the great battle against drink in this country must be careful to lay this to heart. The consideration of this must keep us at once humble as regards our own practice, and charitable in our judgment of others.' Many other gifts of God might be as easily misused as liquor was – wealth, high station, beauty, eloquence, artistic power; (he might have added the love of women, as many early Tractarians did;) but that did not mean they should be forsworn. They should be used instead for the greater glory of God.

He applied the lesson directly to himself. 'Take the blessing of a good education', he said. 'Surely it is mere ingratitude to God to store up knowledge without doing anything to bestow it on others.' He bestowed all that he had learnt: Housman records the thoroughness with which it was done. 'Whether it was the choir, the schools, district visitors, or confirmation classes, upon each in its turn he concentrated his whole mind, spending and being spent in his Master's service, until his strength broke down under the burden, and he was compelled to resign it to another.'

Barnes had proved no healthier for the Ellertons than it had for the Joneses or the Burtons in the seventeenth century. The bodies of three of the youngest Ellerton children – a baby girl, a boy of five and a boy of three – lie together in a small cemetery on Barnes Common: they were carried off during their father's third Barnes winter by an unidentified epidemic. (Ellerton was nevertheless survived by at least five other children: his eldest son followed him in being nominated, by the same Lord Crewe, to a Cheshire rectory.) Public health in Barnes was not advanced by the lack of drainage. A letter from 'Ratepayer', surprisingly appearing in the parish magazine a few years later, reported: 'Our soil is soaked with sewage; scarcely a week passes without the medical officer having to declare some well unfit for further human use'. But the disease which nearly killed Ellerton himself in 1884 was pleurisy, induced by a cold spring on top of overwork.

When he recovered he resigned the living. The Society for the Propagation of the Gospel had found him a couple of continental chaplaincies for that autumn and winter, in places where the size of the English colony warranted them; and he was able to take his family with him. The first was at Veytaux, at the eastern end of Lake Geneva, where he found 'a very happy and congenial group of English exiles': even there, besides writing letters to his friends about the views encountered on his walks, he copied a few items out of Swiss Protestant hymn-books. The second was at Pegli, outside Genoa, where the landlady's modest charge covered 'two bottles of excellent wine' a day, and Ellerton found that 'my church is overshadowed by a palm instead of a yew-tree': his letters now contained descriptions of Michael Angelo's *Pietà* in the *Albergo dei Poveri* in Genoa, or of Giotto's fresco in Florence of Jesus welcoming the disciple whom he loved to heaven: 'And behind him are the other ten – James's young face looking over his shoulder – Peter almost inclined to press forward even before his Master, but keeping back, only thrusting his arms out saying "Dear John, I must have the next embrace": it brings happy tears to one's eyes.'

Ellerton nevertheless came back to London, in May of 1885, without a job. But Walsham How was now a suffragan bishop in London – suffragans were a new thing – and a great success, though he was so small that he needed a box to stand on in the pulpit. He told an Essex baronet with an empty benefice that 'the best living hymn-writer' was without a post; and Ellerton found himself, for the last seven years of his life, rector of White Roding.

He had a moated, rambling seventeenth-century rectory, and an old church which he liked for being thoroughly English-looking: 'I never see its shingled spire peeping through the elms and limes, or its grey tower with a foreground of cornfields and a background of dark trees, without a fresh pleasure in thinking of it as something full of true English beauty and charm, of which one can never tire. We delight also in our green and very unconventional garden, just one of those which arose before people knew how to separate use from beauty, or to fancy they could be separated: so that you scarcely know where your roses end and your cabbages begin.'

Here, nearly sixty, he could employ his time as his tastes directed. Hort came to see him from Cambridge: they discussed new-found fragments of gospel text. He wrote a tract about the communion service called *The Great Indwelling*, discouraging people from pressing too hard on the question of whether Christ was really present at it or not: it would be 'the sign of a "curious and carnal mind" ', he wrote, 'to speculate upon the manner in which our Lord is pleased to give himself to us in the use of his creatures of bread and wine.' He translated Thomas à Kempis. He wrote the little book in which his own amiable character most clearly shows, called *The Twilight of Life*.

It was printed in very large type: it was designed to en-courage people whose sight and strength were failing with the reminder that there were characteristics of old age which had 'their own beauty and blessedness' – gravity, tolerance, a natural *rapport* with children, time to read and think and pray, the opportunity to give counsel and write letters and take part in local good works. The book acknowledged the scourge of loneliness, but gave firm advice about how to avoid it: be open to new ideas, so people come and discuss their plans and interests with you; and don't be grumpy. 'Be thankful and bright to anyone who comes to see you out of kindness; do not think a friend's visit a good opportunity for complaining of your lot; remember that a person with a grievance is a bugbear to everybody. The more cheerful you show yourself, the less lonely you will be.' Ellerton also bravely warned his readers against too precise expectations of heaven, since we really knew very little about it: 'Weigh carefully all that either the Old or the New Testament says about future blessedness, and you will be struck with the fact that there is very little which can be definitely stated.' Hell, at any rate, he as good as said they could forget about: of the story of Dives and Lazarus, the principal gospel evidence for it, he said: 'We cannot be too cautious in the inferences we draw from that mysterious narrative.' There spoke the disciple of Maurice.

A little of his pastoral experience was distilled into the SPCK's *Manual of Parochial Work for the Use of the Younger Clergy*, which he edited. Of the chapters he himself wrote, parts were more or less technical: at communion, 'Take care that the bread is good, and cut small enough'; or again, 'The words of administration should be said to each communicant separately. The sentence is too long, but that cannot be helped.' Parts, though, were more deliberately pastoral. He gave hints about getting round the Prayer-Book instruction that certain classes of dead – notably suicides and the unbaptized – should be denied the burial service; and he urged that nonconformists, and their ministers, should be gracefully received. 'One who can look back upon a ministry of thirty-five years would most earnestly impress upon his younger brethren the duty and benefit of meeting on such occasions dissenting ministers with proper Christian courtesy. Alas, that such a caution should be still needed.' And he urged tact and gentleness in introducing change, whether in services or decoration. 'A wise parish priest, who knows what things are matters of principle and what of expediency, who sympathizes with his flock, and loves them, and trusts them, will be supported by them in all he desires, if he will but be patient.'

In all this, hymnology was not forgotten. One of his pleasures at White Roding was that the church had a good organ and a sizeable choir – girls in white dresses in the front row, boys and men in surplices behind. Through their help he could hear

again the hymns he was recommending for the 1889 edition of
Ancient and Modern, and those of his own which he gathered into
a volume called *Hymns Original and Translated*.

A high proportion were evening hymns; and now at last his
repeated parallel between the evening of the day and the
evening of life had its application to their author. Late in 1891
he had a stroke. He went to Torquay to recover, and had a
second one. Not much benefited by being made (as Medd had
been) an honorary canon of St Albans, he resigned his living in
the spring of 1893 and died that summer. He was buried where
he died, in Torquay; and at his funeral, which turned into a
kind of hymnologists' congress, no fewer than six of his own
hymns were sung. Among them were 'Saviour, again', 'Now the
labourer's task is o'er', and at the end 'O strength and stay'.

Ellerton was transparently a nice man. His niceness breathes
from the mild, myopic face behind the metal-rimmed spectacles
in his photographs. It rises from the printed page, both in what
he wrote and in what other people wrote about him. 'All good
men loved him', wrote Housman, his old curate, three years
after his death; 'and his friends generally spoke, indeed speak of
him still, as "dear Ellerton".' An incumbent who can make his
curate love him can straightaway lay claim to unusual qualities.
On the evidence, of all the rectors of Barnes who are now beyond
the reach of interview he would have been the easiest to like. It
is no accident that he was also the one who best understood the
right relation between an incumbent and his flock. The man
who followed him at Barnes was not so gifted.

9 'The weary incubus of debt' (1884-1944)

LEWIS LOCHÉE, ELLERTON'S SUCCESSOR, WAS A straightforward high-churchman; and yet his parishioners would not let him build that delight of high-churchmen, a new chancel.

In Barnes as elsewhere, it was the story of the next fifty years at least: men who believed in the special authority of the priesthood were nevertheless kept from exercising it by the growing self-assertiveness of their flock. The worshipping laity were better educated than they had been before, and politically enfranchised on a larger scale, and (in the suburbs) thicker on the ground. At first their weight was felt only in isolated rows about ritualism. Then it slowly reached across the whole apparatus of church government, local and national.

Schooling and the vote might not of themselves have been enough to bring that about. The essential agent of change was money. For the first time, the Church of England found it could not pay for things it wanted to do; and the only people who had the money were volunteer contributors among the laity. Paying the piper, they began – softly, hesitantly – to call the tune.

The change had a further consequence of great importance. The incumbent fell into the position of the actor-manager. He had to please to live. He became preoccupied with the size of the takings. If he could not fill enough seats, and gather the consequent return in the various collections which were his box-office, he could not keep the show on the road. He had to take it off or change it. These were not conditions which made the parish ministry attractive to the scholar or the thinker.

There were London churches in the last quarter of the

Lewis Taswell Lochée

nineteenth century where high ceremony in the chancel – 'bells
and smells', in the scornful low-church phrase – led to rioting in
the pews. An area noted for ritual, and rows, was Pimlico. It
was from a church at Pimlico that Lochée came in 1884 to
Barnes. He was a solemn young man of thirty-five: he had been
educated at Tonbridge and afterwards at Exeter, Oxford (by
then a high-church college). He regularly republished his
sermons in the parish magazine which Ellerton had founded.
He had no time for Ellerton's scepticism about the story of
Dives and Lazarus: indeed, he took the two of them to have
been historical characters, men about Jerusalem just before
Jesus told the story. 'There was something about the two, so
lately familiar figures, but now missing in Jerusalem, which
they did not know as yet', said Lochée of Jesus's hearers, 'but
which, because it would be good for them to know, he now goes
on to tell them' – and that was the two men's subsequent
adventures in the after-life, taken to be equally historical. In
another sermon he assumed that the parable of the good
Samaritan, too, had been 'the story of an occurrence which
possibly recently had happened'. Lochée's life had the same
plodding quality as his sermons. A curate remembered him as
punctual, exact and earnest.

He early conceived the plan of enlarging the parish church
with a chancel. The north aisle had been added piecemeal over
the past hundred years, and it was still not the same length as
the medieval south aisle. Lochée proposed to make it the main
axis of the church: he would turn all its seats, which he found
'maze-like', to face the front, and at the empty eastern end he
would add a chancel. He had plans drawn by an experienced
architect, James St Aubyn. These he announced as something
that was going to happen, not as a matter for discussion: it was
what he had determined to do, and he felt sure that mere
knowledge of that fact would enlist his parishioners' active
sympathy. He reminded them of David's advice (at I Chronicles
22.5) to Solomon, adding his own italics: 'The house that is to
be builded for the Lord must be *exceeding magnifical*.'

Lochée wanted the chancel as a climactic religious symbol.
'Of all the accessories of divine worship which, as being her

lawful inheritance, the English Church is gradually winning back,' he wrote to a parishioner, 'none, to me at any rate, is more full of teaching than a procession, conducted as it should be – following the Cross in its progress through the world, and at length reaching heaven, which the chancel symbolizes.' But to a stoutly low-church element in his flock the chancel symbolized something a great deal simpler: creeping popery, and the undue exaltation of the priestly function. Two rancorous public meetings voted the plan down; and whatever the rector's rights, without local support he had no chance of raising the £2500 which the scheme would have cost. He was given to understand that if he wanted extra space the most he could do was build a permanent church in place of Ellerton's tin tabernacle. A site beyond the railway-line was duly bought, and one of Lochée's own churchwardens appointed architect; but Lochée himself died before a brick was laid. He was forty-one. The cause of his death was found to be typhoid fever; but his supporters freely claimed that the low-church faction had killed him, since the worry it caused him had weakened his resistance to disease. Party battles in 1891 were still fought with whatever ammunition came to hand.

He had a successor, William Anthony Harrison, who was in the rectory little more than seven months before he too was carried off, early in 1892. Harrison was a clever man (he had taken a first in moral sciences at that low-church Cambridge college, Caius, thirty-five years before) worn out by a quarter-century of parish work in Lambeth; and he only had time to appeal for money to pay his two curates properly before he declined into his last illness. So in effect the next rector after Lochée was Benjamin Meredyth Kitson, inducted on the same day in 1892 that the foundation-stone was laid of the permanent church in Westfields – St Michaels.' It was Westfields, with its mean straight streets where diphtheria was endemic, which created most of the work for which curates were wanted.

Kitson's thirty-year run encapsulated the problems of the Church of England on the ground, even though it succeeded for a while in concealing them. Kitson knew all about the shortage of money for curates. After an undistinguished under-

Benjamin Meredyth Kitson

graduate career at Queen's, Oxford, where he was a rowing man, and curacies in Manchester and Pimlico, he had been an organizing secretary for the Additional Curates Society. It raised money to pay for curates in parishes where funds could not be found from the incumbent's salary, or his private means, or the diocese, or local subscription. Kitson then did a brief stint with the Additional Bishoprics Fund – during the 1880s new dioceses had been endowed in the populous north of England, but there was still a need for more, as later change acknowledged – before he became the vicar of a newish church at Clapton, in north-east London.

A visitor remembered the Clapton church as having been at first 'as bare as a barn – a striking contrast to the sumptuous, richly-furnished fane which Mr Kitson left on his coming to Barnes twelve years later'. Kitson was a late-Victorian high-churchman: he had his period's love of complicated interior decoration, at church as well as home. He greatly approved the Lincoln judgment of 1890, in which Archbishop Benson of Canterbury had upheld – and been upheld two years later by the Privy Council for upholding – certain high-church practices complained of in Bishop King. (They included lighted candles on the altar and the 'eastward position', in which the priest had his back to the congregation.) Kitson was incensed by the famous papal bull of 1894 (never yet withdrawn) in which Leo XIII declared Anglican orders 'absolutely null and utterly void'; but his comfort was that it would put a stop to the unworthy taunt that if a clergyman tried to 'improve his services' he was going over to Rome. 'It will now be seen that such intentions or unions are simply impossible, and that we only wish to present the teaching and ritual of the Church of England in all their fullness, and in obedience to the plain directions of the Prayer Book, and that this means the most intense loyalty to the Church of England.'

Kitson was a bluff, bonhomous bachelor with short hair and a powerful voice. Striding the parish in shovel hat and inverness cape, he had a jocular but telling fashion of asking stray parishioners why they had not been in church on Sunday. He was a popular figure – energetic, good at putting people at their

ease, a capable chairman. He became rural dean (a title
already absurd – it meant leader among a handful of suburban
clergy). For the last four years of his life he was an honorary
canon of Southwark. It was believed among his flock that he
had twice refused a colonial bishopric.

He was no intellectual. In a period when the work of the
German theologian Adolf Harnack had reopened for many
English churchmen the question of Christ's divinity, Kitson
believed that the proper attitude in face of awkward doctrines
was uncomprehending awe. In one of the very few sermons he
had reprinted in the parish magazine, in 1913, he said of the
doctrine of the Trinity: 'It transcends all human thought. We
have no language, no comparison that will aid us. It is a sheer,
adamantine cliff, against which the waves of human thought
may surge for ever, and not displace one fragment.'

Nearly all his interventions in the parish magazine were
appeals for money. 'I earnestly trust that the comparatively
small sum asked for will soon be guaranteed.' 'The solution of
this problem must rest with you and not with me.' 'I trust that
this Christmas will see the extinction of the weary incubus of
debt.' The economy of the parish was sustained by a multiplicity of small funds, each separately subscribed to and
administered. By 1913 there were over thirty Two of them,
unimpressively supported, were for foreign missions, and one
for home missions; but the bulk of them were for use no further
away than Westfields.

There were funds for a parish nurse, and a coal club, and a
clothing club, and a women's provident society, and a children's
shoe club, and a women's boot club, and a blanket club, and a
soup kitchen, and children's dinners, and working men's social
evenings, and a maternity society. A couple of the funds were
for bricks and mortar. Streetfuls of new parishioners were being
added all the time: the church meadows were sold for houses,
and the rector was commemorated in a Kitson Road and a
Meredyth Road before his term in the parish was half over.
(Melvill and Ellerton were similarly remembered, by their
surnames; Melvill's was mis-spelt.) In consequence, besides
carrying through the building of St Michael's, Kitson felt

justified in 1905 in greatly extending the parish church. His architect was the same churchwarden again, by this time aged eighty; and because Kitson added a whole third aisle, he had no difficulty about slipping in a new chancel as well.

A constant item was a fund to pay the curates who would man these many enterprises. There were often three of them; sometimes four. Being unmarried, and having a little money of his own, Kitson could run the rectory as a clergymen's mess. All decisions were taken from there. Some of his lieutenants were drawn to him by his known views and energy, and stayed a dozen years or more. One of them enlivened endless issues of the magazine with choirboy-howler jokes. ('Who was Noah's wife?' 'Joan of Arc.') One of them served for three years without any pay at all. One of them, as a chaplain to the forces in the First World War, won the Military Cross on the western front for tending the wounded under fire.

That war made on the face of it very little difference to this system, under which the clergy appeared for the moment to be defying modernity by running the show their own way on the money of the laity. In July 1914 Bishop Reginald Copleston, who had been bishop of Calcutta, came to Barnes to preach. He had been born in the rectory, the eldest son of the nineteenth-century rector of the same name; his brother Ernest became bishop of Colombo. The bishop, preaching at what was taken to be the church's seven hundredth anniversary, was eloquent on 'the reality of progress in human things, where these are under the influence of Christianity'. It looks now like a classic of episcopal fatuity: a month later came the war which demolished that kind of optimism for good. Yet for a while it almost seemed as if the bishop might be right. Little changed. There was still a curate to give away the prizes at the kindergarten treat. The lengthening list of the parish's war dead was read out in church each Sunday; but the Mothers' Union could still hold its annual social meeting and tea under the copper beech in the rectory garden. The eternal values were safe.

The bubble burst when Kitson died in 1923. His chosen activities were then seen to have been just as dependent as Lochée's on money given by parishioners. Kitson's authoritarian

charm had pulled it in, but not in large enough amounts: the
gap had been filled only partly from his own contributions and
through the personal privations of his underpaid curates. The
last two of that band were now departed: one of them – Kitson's
own nephew – had gone to be the first vicar of St Michael's when
it became a separate parish in 1919, and the other melted away
on Kitson's death. Congregations dwindled. Clubs collapsed.
The most revealing emblem of change and decay was the rectory
itself, momentarily emptied. For years there had been no money
to maintain it. Its serenity was a sham. It was discovered to
show advanced signs of bachelor dilapidation. Kitson's successor
wrote publicly of his shock at its deplorable state of neglect.

   This degree of poverty in the established Church, this gross
disparity between ends and means, had a number of causes.
One of them was all the building and extending of churches
which a moving and growing population called for. Another
was the women's boot club and the children's dinners: in the
long interval between the acknowledgment of the case for a
Welfare State (signalled by the Liberal reform programme begun
in 1905) and its establishment in the late 1940s, the parish
church saw a duty to act, and its means would not stretch. For
the same reason, ecclesiastical bureaucracy multiplied, and
parishes had to pay for that, too: between the wars the diocesan
quota (part of which went to national headquarters at Church
House in Westminster) became a significant burden on parish
economies. At the same time, incumbents were growing less and
less able to come to the rescue from their own purse. In part
because of the steady increase in taxation, and in part because
the status of the clergy was declining with its autocracy, there
were fewer and fewer of them who had private means. In
Barnes, Lochée and Kitson were effectively the last to have an
income of their own, and it did not stretch far. Clerical salaries
were themselves diminishing in real terms, as the return on the
investments which provided them lost ground to the cost of
living. A salary of £417 a year at the beginning of the century,
as in Barnes, was nothing like so comfortable when it had risen
only to £578 twenty-five years later. (After the Second World
War, inflation bore even more hardly on such comparatively

good livings: with the Church of England's funds increasingly centralized, its finance men concentrated on raising the lower salaries while the higher ones hardly moved, so that in the end something near uniformity reigned.)

The new rector, Patrick Dott, was a man in his early fifties whose second curacy, after Oriel, Oxford, had been at Edward Layfield's old church of All Hallows: from there he had gone to be a missionary in South Africa, and then a mission fund-raiser in the York diocese, before he moved to a Croydon parish and thence to Barnes. Since he was both small in stature and strange in manner, his name was the subject of a number of more or less obvious local jokes. In Barnes he made little of his mission past. Interest in the conversion of the distant heathen had become, for the mass of English worshippers, perfunctory: in the early years of the century there had been a branch of the Coral League in the parish – the junior arm of the Universities' Mission to Central Africa, enrolling children of five and upwards for a subscription of threepence a year; but even that had sunk into inactivity.

Dott was a high-churchman like Kitson and Lochée. He saw differences in churchmanship as differences largely of temperament, and accepted his bishop's reminder that 'the Church must be comprehensive'; but his own sympathies were clear in the changes he advocated. 'The Anglo-Catholic', he wrote, 'possesses in a high degree the sense of the sacramental. Ritual, ornament, the outward gesture of priest and people are an actual part of the thing signified. By and through them he communicates with God. Without them religion seems to him a mutilated thing, deprived alike of beauty and reality.'

Like Lochée, Dott tried to pull the parish's practices a little nearer that end of the scale, and failed. His congregation was beginning to sense that its veto powers extended not just to special building projects but to the whole range of church observances. Dott early decided that the main Sunday morning service, at any rate on two Sundays a month, should be a parish communion – not just matins, but matins leading into a choral communion service. 'During the last forty or so years', he wrote, 'a strong movement had been on foot in our Church to restore

(for that is the right word) the holy communion service to its
central place as the chief service for Christian worshippers.' He
was right that it was a widespread movement, and over the next
forty years it carried its way widely; but not without a good deal
of low-church grumbling. The change came in the end to be
recognized as giving the congregation a bigger part in the
service than before, and therefore diminishing rather than
increasing the separateness and dominance of the priestly caste;
but in 1927 in Barnes, as in many other places, the move was
regarded as merely priest-instigated and high-church. Dott
tried the change; but within a year he had first modified and
then scrapped it.

There was a parliamentary parallel over the revised Prayer
Book. After the rows over ritual at the turn of the century, a
Royal Commission on Ritual Matters had been appointed in
1904: as a result of its report the work of revising the Prayer
Book was put in hand, and by 1927 the revision was ready. It
sanctioned most of the existing departures from the 1662 ordinance; they were broadly in a high-church direction. The two
Convocations passed the book; but – since this was still the
Church of England as by law established – Parliament's approval was needed too. The Lords gave their assent; but the
Commons refused it, and repeated their refusal in 1928. Not all
the MPs who voted the book down were believing Anglicans:
one of them, notoriously, was a Communist Parsee; but they
saw that the backers of the change were mostly clerics, they
perceived the virulence of the low-church fear that the Church
of England was being tilted dangerously towards its high-church
side, and they discharged their representative function accordingly.

Dott had welcomed the new book, as making people 'less
content to abide in the mists and damps of lower life'. He was
particularly pleased that it proposed to allow a practice which
the old book had disallowed, reserving the sacrament (keeping
consecrated bread and wine in a safe place for later use elsewhere – convenient for administering to the sick, but suggesting
the Roman view that the priest in consecrating the elements had
been able to make them somehow magically different). He now

seemed to accept defeat. 'The time for discussing what is to be used is over. The time for putting to its best use what has been given has arrived.' But it soon became clear that to him and to many other priests, encouraged by most of their bishops, 'what had been given' included the revised book. Within three years Dott was mooting reserved sacraments and parish communions once again.

The forces of the time were against him. For a few years now he had had to contend with a Parochial Church Council, notionally elected by all the baptized Anglicans in the parish: it was the bottom brick in a complicated four-tier system of accountability in the Church of England established in principle at the end of the First World War, in the same flush of feeling that greatly extended the political franchise. Its powers were vague and ill-understood; but essentially they could only grow, because the Council's existence expressed the new reality of the century – that the Church wanted money as never before, and only the laity had it, and they could not be expected to give it up for nothing for ever.

Dott wanted money for a church hall. It was eventually built at the foot of the rectory lawn, beyond the copper beech. The architect was the rector's wife. (To be scrupulously fair, she had some training in the discipline.) The total cost, £4000, took the parishioners more than five years to raise; and they had barely finished when they were called on to find another £2500 for restoration work to the church itself. They began to be overwhelmed. By the early 1930s they were regularly defaulting on their annual quota for the diocese, and discontent was rife. Dott himself detected 'an evil spirit of carping and unrest'.

The symbolic problem of the rectory remained unresolved. Like the office of rector itself as the incumbents of that time understood it, it stood shoulder to shoulder with the church, apparently tranquil in its domination of the community, in fact living with the threat of collapse. Its lawn was the scene of increasingly frantic attempts at fund-raising: Dott gave a number of garden-parties for dogs. He was the sixteenth rector to live in the house since it was built in 1717; and he and his wife never overcame the problems of its endlessly varying floor-levels, its

top-floor flat for the curate and his family with no separate
access, its searching draughts. The seventeenth rector to live
there, Robert Curwen, was the last.

He also happened to be, for the time being, the last of an even
longer run of rectors who had been educated at Oxford or
Cambridge, going back at least to Thomas Jones in 1614.
Curwen had been at Oxford in the late 1890s. He came to
Barnes as the result of a swap. Dott had tried to achieve release
from his recalcitrant congregation through an exchange with a
City incumbent in 1933, but the deal collapsed; he managed it
in 1936 with Curwen, a man of about sixty who had been in
parish work in the southern counties ever since he left Wadham
and Cuddesdon. He was now at Winterslow, on the London
side of Salisbury. So Dott went to spend the last two years of his
life in a straggling agricultural community in eastern Wiltshire;
and Curwen, no more than five years his junior, came to live in
the house that Francis Hare had built.

Curwen was in the image of the house's exterior: tall, stately.
He was not a complainer, but he acknowledged after a while
that 'its interior arrangement is extraordinarily inconvenient
and old-fashioned, and lacking in all the modern improvements
which make domestic life possible nowadays'. The Parochial
Church Council had no money to spare: the diocesan quota was
still not being paid in full; but Curwen decided that rebuilding
the house inside was preferable to knocking it down and
building a smaller one (which would involve – he had a
matching stateliness of phrase – 'utilizing part of the rectory
ground for what is known as development'). The round of
garden fetes and collections began again; about a quarter of the
needed £2500 was raised; the rector, the curate and their
families decamped; work actually began, just reaching the
point where the rector could report in the parish magazine 'at
present the interior can only be described as a devastated area'.
But the date of that issue was September 1939. Nothing more
was done throughout the Second World War. Curwen spent
another five years in Barnes without ever going back to the
rectory again. After the war the house was sold (and preserved),
and a smaller one bought. Curwen's successors lived in a semi-

detached Edwardian villa like most of their parishioners. Something of the mystique of the office had been shed for good.

It happened in other places too. All over the country, incumbents were being driven from the parsonage by economics, just as three hundred years before they had been pushed out by politics. From Cutts to Curwen, these twenty-five rectors of one parish typified their times. In the seventeenth century they exemplified the rival rigidities which ended in the first major free-church migration from the Church of England. In the eighteenth they showed the erastianism, the submission to secular authority and standards, which helped determine the second, Methodist, departure. They returned in the nineteenth century to the worship of God; but a synthesis between the religion of the individual heart and the religion of the professionals continued to escape them; and the twentieth century found them still struggling to impose expert authority on a world less and less minded to obedience. The rectors of Barnes, standing for a multitude of incumbents in many periods and places, help to make that story humanly comprehensible.

At first sight, the conclusion which arises from it is comforting. Most things have happened before. 'Is there anything whereof it may be said, See, this is new? It hath been already of old time, which was before us.' The first chapter of Ecclesiastes puts the point a little strongly; but these brief lives support the same suggestion. Few of the phenomena which make late-twentieth-century Anglicans uneasy are new. Divisions are not new. Scepticism about the creeds is not new. Fervent upholding or rejection of the symbolic importance of the priesthood is not new. Even clerical poverty is not new (though it is true that the rare peaks of clerical wealth have been toppled only this century). Decidedly, unfitness for their office among incumbents is not new. On the whole, there is a case for saying that things are at any rate no worse than they used to be.

On the other hand, in absolute terms the recital is – like much Christian history – disheartening. It shows Anglican parsons to have been often worldly, often obscurantist, often baselessly authoritarian. It almost constitutes a new argument for the existence of God: if the flock could survive pastors like some of these, there must have been a God to guide it. Even in comparative terms, too, parts of the picture are unencouraging. It is difficult to deny the evidence of decline in the clergy's intellectual quality. Between 1680 and 1876, among the thirteen rectors who came to Barnes there were seven who had been Oxford or Cambridge dons. There have been none since. Many other parishes could show comparable figures. A less specialized test – the ability to write publishable work – would give the same result.

It may well be that though clergymen are in the main less intelligent and instructed than they have sometimes been, they are also holier. The worldliness of many eighteenth-century clerics in particular is an offence with which their twentieth-century successors cannot be charged. Religion is an assertion of the transcendental and the eternal. A preoccupation with temporalities debases it; and that has largely gone. In an era when a bishop is paid less than – for example – almost any London journalist, few men enter the ministry with an eye to material betterment. You could read in that very fact the explanation of intellectual decline: inadequate money draws inadequate men. But that would be to take a dispiritingly low view of the religious life, and one not borne out by observation. It would be to suggest that the chief stimulus by which religious-minded people are stirred is money. The evidence of countless faithful households runs quite the other way. Low pay may have its effect on recruitment to the ministry at the margin; but as a reason for a marked lessening in intellectual weight it is not by itself enough.

The decline has much less to do with worldliness than with the other two propensities which our story discloses: obscurantism and authoritarianism. Obscurantism, the willingness to see free enquiry stifled, is an enemy to whole-hearted worship. Religion must witness to the transcendental, yes; but it must also live in the world of its own day. It must take steady account of advances in human knowledge. One of the scandals of the intellectual life of this country in the past century has been the sustained pretence – in which the Church of England has been joined by almost every other Church – that the content of Christian belief can remain exactly what it was in a pre-scientific age, when belief of all kinds depended on statements from an exalted source rather than on reasoned enquiry. The professionals have known for a century and a half of the modifications in belief made unavoidable by discoveries in the sciences, in history, in biblical criticism, in comparative religion; and yet they have not preached them. They are not preaching them yet. There is a dishonesty here, a disregard for the divine attribute of truth, which has given long offence to thinking people. It has kept a great many of them out of the pews. It must also have stopped a good number from compounding the dishonesty by taking to the pulpit.

Equally effective in keeping thoughtful aspirants away has been authoritarianism. The incumbent who folds his arms and declares that by virtue of his ordination he knows best – and he is still a familiar figure – is in retreat from reason. He is seeking to return to the time when authority was enough; and there is no road back. Whatever its historical springs among the Tractarians and the Carolines, that yearning now represents parsonical worldliness in a transferred form. Stripped of the status conferred on him by comparative affluence, the incumbent claims instead the mysterious superiority of the priest. He does himself and his profession a disservice. In an age when authority has to be earned, the claim is troubling to the onlooker. He sees incumbents who cannot carry the part they have themselves chosen. They are imprisoned in loneliness by the barrier it sets between them and other people; believing that anything they choose to do is directed by a higher power, they are corrupted into doing nothing; they are depressed to the verges of insanity by the gap between their expectations from their special magic and its barely perceptible achievements. It is not an example the observer wishes to follow.

The effect on congregations is yet more discouraging – and more important, since a church is the whole company of its faithful and not just its professional staff. You can say, of course, that lay people are at fault in letting clerical authoritarianism strike root: it is up to them to see that the divine right of priests goes the same way as the divine right of kings. But they are uncertain of their ground, and anxious to avoid rows; and so they simply stay away instead. It is an oddity of the Church of England that nothing has so great an influence on the size of congregations as the character of the incumbent. It ought not to be so, given the comparative fixity of Anglican forms of service: as long as both can read aloud, one man's conduct of worship ought to be much the same as another's. Roman Catholics seem to manage to go to church, or stay away, without the aptitudes of the parish priest being much of a consideration. But Catholics are great believers in the sole efficacy of the sacraments: Protestants value at least as much the ministry of the word. They ask to be allowed to use their wits. An incumbent who prevents that – who preaches a Sunday-school biblicism, who seeks to preserve all decisions about the management of the church and its pastoral activity in his own hands – is keeping numbers of them from the worship and the service they need. Confusing the church with himself, he diminishes the church.

What sort of figure, then, ought to be the pattern for late-twentieth-century parsons? When a sequel to this book comes to be written in a hundred years' time, who will deserve the writer's and the reader's admiration?

He – or she – will be a servant of God. As such, his rank among his own parishioners will have little interest for him. The standing which comes with wealth he will never have expected; but he will disclaim, too, any special status as the steward of a mystery. Wherever he can, in the church's affairs, he will discern the talent in members of his congregation and enable them to use it. He will know his own, and trust them. Even in the sphere of worship and doctrine he will press his own judgment only sparingly, and submit it from time to time to the unofficial audit of his congregation's approval. As a sign, he will at the outset voluntarily divest himself of the parson's freehold, his peculiar impregnability to dismissal: he will undertake to reopen the question of his future at set intervals. He will thus be, and be seen to be, as other men are; and the release from any implicit claim to superhuman capacities will do much for his usefulness and contentment.

But the chief expression of his love of God will be a love of truth. He will already be an educated man, able to follow an argument and to set it out intelligibly in the written and the spoken word. He will keep up his reading in theology and the related disciplines, laying the fruits of it constantly before his parishioners, so that they can keep or learn a faith which has point for the world they live in. He will give thanks for congregations and incumbents of the past, for the continuity of belief which has brought him to that place; but his eye will be on the believers of his own time. In all this, being human, he will fall short; yet even to attempt it will earn him an honourable place in his church's history.

A note on sources

I owe much to manuscript notes on the rectors of Barnes compiled over many years by Mary Grimwade, of the Barnes and Mortlake History Society, in particular from act books and wills in Lambeth Palace library; and to a typescript history of Barnes parish church completed in 1950 by Arthur Lever, using church registers and vestry books.

The *Dictionary of National Biography*, besides carrying entries for Burton, Hare, Warner, Melvill and Medd, covers most of the surrounding cast. Of general histories I have used J. W. C. Wand, *A History of the Modern Church* (3rd edn 1938); Williston Walker, *A History of the Christian Church* (revised edn, New York 1959); J. J. Tayler, *A Retrospect of the Religious Life of England* (2nd edn 1876); H. O. Wakeman, *The History of the Church of England* (3rd edn 1897); J. H. R. Moorman, *A History of the Church in England* (3rd edn 1973); and the last seven volumes of the *Oxford History of England*.

For the nineteenth century I have been greatly helped by Owen Chadwick, *The Victorian Church* (2 vols.: part 1, 3rd edn 1971; part 2, 2nd edn 1972). I have also consulted Roger Dixon and Stefan Muthesius, *Victorian Architecture* (1978); and – for the period since 1870 – successive issues of *Crockford's Clerical Directory*.

Those general aids aside, my main written sources for each chapter have been these:

Chapter 1 (*Cutts, Rutton, Lenthall, Griffith, Squire, Layfield, Burton*):

A. G. Matthews, *Walker Revised, being a revision of John Walker's sufferings of the clergy during the Grand Rebellion, 1642–60* (1948), and *Calamy Revised, being a revision of Edmund Calamy's Account of the Ministers and others ejected and silenced, 1660–2* (1934); W. A. Shaw, *History of the English Church 1640–60* (2 vols, 1900); Survey of London vol. 12, *The Parish of All Hallows Barking* (1929); Hezekiah Burton, *Several Discourses*, with preface by John Tillotson (2 vols, 1684–5); Anthony à Wood, *Athenae Oxonienses*, ed. Philip Bliss (1813–20) (vol. 4, on Tillotson and Burton); Thomas Birch, *Life of Dr John Tillotson* (1753); Matthew Sylvester, ed., *Reliquiae Baxterianae* (1696); Daniel Neal, *History of the Puritans 1517–1688* (1822).

Chapter 2 (*Richardson, Hare, Kilborn, Baker*):

Francis Hare, *Works* (4 vols, 1746); Jonathan Swift, *Examiner*, 11 January 1710 and 15 February 1711, *A Learned Comment upon Dr Hare's Excellent Sermon* (1711), *The Conduct of the Allies* (1711) (all in Clarendon Press edn, vol. 3, 1940), and *Remarks on the Barrier Treaty* (1712) (vol. 6, 1951); Augustus J. C. Hare, *Memorials of a Quiet Life* (3 vols, 1872); Lord Hervey, *Memoirs of the Reign of George the Second*, ed. J. W. Croker (1848) (ch. xxiii); H. H. Milman, *Annals of St Paul's Cathedral* (2nd edn 1869); literary references to Hare at Pope, *Dunciad*, iii 204, and Thackeray, *Esmond*, bk ii, ch. 7; Robert Kilborn, sermons preached in 1728 and 1729.

Chapter 3 (*Hume*):

the Newcastle papers in the British Library; John Hume, sermons preached in 1747, 1757, and two in 1762; Stephen Hyde Cassan, *Lives and Memoirs of the Bishops of Sherborne and Salisbury* (1824); W. H. R. Jones, *Fasti Ecclesiae Sarisberiensis* (1879).

Chapter 4 (*Warner*):

the Newcastle papers; Ferdinando Warner, sermons preached in 1729 and 1737, *A System of Divinity and Morality* (5 vols, 1750), *A Rational Defence of the English Reformation and Protestant Religion* (1752), *An Illustration of the Book of Common Prayer* (1754), *Bolingbroke* (1755), *A Free and Necessary Enquiry* (1755), *Memoirs* of the Life of Sir Thomas More (1758), The History of England as it relates to Religion and the Church (2 vols, 1759), Advice from a Bishop (1760), A Scheme for a Fund (1752), An Address to the Clergy with some proposals for raising and establishing a Fund (1755), Letter to the Fellows of Sion College (1764), The History of Ireland (1763), The History of the Rebellion and Civil War in Ireland (1767), and A Full and Plain Account of the Gout (1768).

Chapter 5 (Wilson, Jeffreys, Jeffreys, Copleston):

the Newcastle papers; Christopher Wilson, sermons preached in 1754 and 1785; Alumni Cantabrigienses iv (to 1751) and Gloucestershire Notes and Queries viii (1901) (for Wilson's biographical details); Daniel Lysons, The Environs of London (4 vols, 2nd edn 1811); William Hone, The Year Book (1832); R. B. Beckett, Hogarth (1949); W. J. Copleston, Memoir of Edward Copleston (1851); Geoffrey Faber, Oxford Apostles (2nd edn 1936).

Chapter 6 (Melvill):

Noel Annan, Leslie Stephen (1951); Ford K. Brown, Fathers of the Victorians (1961); Ian Bradley, The Call to Seriousness (1976); Memoirs of the late Philip Melvill (1812); Henry Melvill, Sermons (2 vols, 1833 and 1838), Sermons preached at Cambridge in 1836, 1837 and 1839, Sermons on certain of the less prominent facts and references in Sacred Story (2 vols, 1843 and 1845), Miscellaneous Sermons iii (selected from the Pulpit and mostly preached at Camden Chapel 1843–4), A Selection from the Lectures delivered at St Margaret's, Lothbury, 1850–52 (1853), Sermons delivered in the Cathedral Church of St Paul, selected from the Penny Pulpit (1860), and Selection from the Sermons preached during the latter years of his life in the parish church of Barnes and in the Cathedral of St Paul's. with memoir, (2 vols, 1872); A Parishioner, The Reverend Mr Melvill's Political Sermon (1835); Henry Crabb Robinson, Diary, ed. Thomas Sadler (2 vols, 3rd edn 1872); Thomas Babington Macaulay and others, The Indian Civil Service (1855); F. C. Danvers, Sir Monier Monier-Williams and others, Memorials of Old Haileybury College (1894); J. O. Johnston, Life and Letters of Henry Parry Liddon (1905); William Sinclair, Memorials of St Paul's Cathedral (1909).

Chapter 7 (*Medd*):

James Bentley, *Ritualism and Politics in Victorian Britain* (1978); P. G. Medd, *The Priest to the Altar* (privately printed, 1860), *Household Prayer* (1864), 'Sacerdotalism', *Church Quarterly Review* (unsigned) (first issue, October, 1875), *Sermons preached in the Parish Church of Barnes, 1871 to 1876* (1877), *The One Mediator* (1884), and *Letters of William Bright*, ed. B. J. Kidd, with memoir by P. G. Medd (1903); obituary notices in the *Wiltshire and Gloucestershire Standard* and the *Cheltenham and Gloucestershire Graphic Chronicle* for 1 August 1908; manuscript diary, letters, notebooks, prayer-books, sermons and photographs kindly made available by Edward Nesbitt Medd of Chertsey (a surviving son).

Chapter 8 (*Ellerton*):

John Ellerton, sermon preached at Crewe Hall in 1870, *The Holiest Manhood and its lessons for busy lives – sermons preached in Barnes Church* (1882), *The Twilight of Life* (1886), *Manual of Parochial Work* (with others) (1888, new edn 1892), and *The Great Indwelling* (1890); Henry Housman, *John Ellerton: being a collection of his writings on hymnology, together with a sketch of his life and works* (1896); John Julian, *Dictionary of Hymnology* (2nd edn 1907); *Hymns Ancient and Modern Revised* (1972 reprint); Edward Asling, *The Story of St Michael and All Angels, Barnes* (1928); Barnes parish magazine, 1877, 1884.

Chapter 9 (*Lochée, Harrison, Kitson, Dott, Curwen*):

Asling, *St Michael's*; Barnes parish magazine, 1884–1944; vestry and Parochial Church Council minutes.

Except where indicated in the text, I have standardized spelling, punctuation and the use of capital letters, in order that quaintness shall not stand in the way of the sense or obscure the essential modernity of the points at issue.

Table of rectors and monarchs

	1625 Charles I
1635 John Cutts	
1643 Thomas Rutton	
1647 Robert Lenthall	
	1649 (The Commonwealth)
1658 G. Griffith	
1660 John Squire	1660 Charles II
1662 Edward Layfield	
1680 Hezekiah Burton	
1681 William Richardson	
	1685 James II
	1689 William III and Mary
	1702 Anne
	1714 George I
1717 Francis Hare	
1727 Robert Kilborn	1727 George II
1730 Samuel Baker	
1749 John Hume	
1758 Ferdinando Warner	
	1760 George III
1768 Christopher Wilson	
1792 John Jeffreys senior	
1795 John Jeffreys junior	
	1820 George IV
	1830 William IV
	1837 Victoria
1840 Reginald Copleston	
1863 Henry Melvill	
1870 Peter Goldsmith Medd	
1876 John Ellerton	
1884 Lewis Taswell Lochée	
1891 William Anthony Harrison	
1892 Benjamin Meredyth Kitson	
	1901 Edward VII
	1910 George V
1923 William Patrick Dott	
1936 Robert Moncrieff Curwen	1936 Edward VIII
	1936 George VI

Index